UNDER THE SHADE OF OLIVE TREES

Recipes from Jerusalem to Marrakech
AND BEYOND

Nadia Zerouali & Merijn Tol

Photography Sven Benjamins   **Illustration and Design** Rosa Vitalie

STEWART, TABORI & CHANG
NEW YORK

Published in 2014 by Stewart, Tabori & Chang
An imprint of ABRAMS

Library of Congress Control Number:
2013945653

ISBN: 978-1-61769-108-9

Editor: Holly Dolce
Designer: Sebit Min
Production Manager: Anet Sirna-Bruder

The text of this book was composed in
Lydian, FF Scala, FF Scala Sans.

Printed and bound in China

10 9 8 7 6 5 4 3 2 1

Stewart, Tabori & Chang books are available at special discounts when purchased in
quantity for premiums and promotions as well
as fundraising or educational use. Special
editions can also be created to specification.
For details, contact specialsales@abrams-
books.com or the address below.

THE ART OF BOOKS SINCE 1949

115 West 18th Street
New York, NY 10011
www.abramsbooks.com

• PREFACE •

What is Arabic cuisine? We like to take a broad view. For us, it encompasses all of the rich, ancient cuisines of the Middle East, ancient Persian-Arabic cuisine, ancient Ottoman and Turkish cuisine, the cuisines from the countries surrounding the Mediterranean Sea (including the Arabic influences in Spain and Italy), the cuisines from the Maghreb countries (Morocco, Algeria, Tunisia, and Libya), and the influences they had elsewhere.

Just when we were making plans for a new culinary forage in the Arabic world, we realized that we still had so much in our heads, belies, and hearts that we needed to begin by making a book at home: a book in which every lover of the rich Arabic cuisine in our homeland could find a clear explanation and illustration of the flavors, ingredients, and recipes from our beloved Arabia.

We started referring to this region of the world as Arabia during our journey, by car, from Beirut to Damascus. Arabic is the language that binds the people throughout the Arabic world, a world with many countries, each with a contemporary, colorful, and delicious collection of peoples and cultures.

And just like the Arabic influence traveled with the Moors from Spain to the Netherlands in the form of almond paste–filled phyllo dough rolls, *kruidnootjes* (small cinnamon-nutmeg-gingerbread–like cookies), and *hutspot* (a Dutch carrot-potato stew), that influence is now visible everywhere in our country, in the cities but also in smaller villages, in the form of new neighborhood delis. Tahini and flat-leaf parsley are readily available in your Turkish and Moroccan groceries.

The tastes of the various cuisines

Middle Eastern cuisine is characterized by sour, fresh, zesty, and aromatic flavors in the form of yogurt, sumac, lemon, parsley, mint, dill, and many raw, vegetables.

The Maghreb cuisines are spice filled, with contrast in sweet and salty flavors. Many spices with sweet flavors are combined with hearty, fermented flavors like candied lemon and smen; dried subtropical fruit, nuts, parsley, mint, and cilantro are usually not used raw.

In Mediterranean cuisine, one finds influences from the cuisines mentioned above, with ingredients like couscous, almonds, parsley, spices, and citrus. The sweet pastries and cookies from the Arabs remain especially present in the modern Mediterranean cuisine.

This book is an ode to all those products and hopefully an invitation to indulge in these rich cuisines and cultures. In this book you'll find real Arabia recipes and traditional recipes from Lebanon, Iraq, Spain, Morocco, Israel, Yemen, Tunisia, Syria, Jordan, Bahrain, Afghanistan, Turkey, Iran, and Italy. We are incredibly happy to have grown up in the Netherlands, among the delicious foods that originally stem from all these cuisines: all flavors and ingredients are nearby. Yet because we are Dutch, we can operate freely while remaining conscious of tradition and recipes. We aren't bound by borders—the ingredients provide the directions. *Bismilla, sahtein!*

> *You carry all the ingredients*
> *To turn your existence into joy.*
> *Mix them,*
> *Mix them!*
> Hafiz, Persian Sufi poet from the thirteenth century

Eating in the Arabic world

Abundance! No need to call at 5:30 p.m. to ask if they can prepare an extra serving. At the Arabic table there's always room for at least ten people if necessary. It wouldn't occur to a cook in Arabia to prepare a measured amount of food. Leftovers? You'll make your neighbors, friends, and family happy. And you'll make new friends. Once we were accused of making quantities that could feed an entire soccer team. Yes, that's true, and we do it with pleasure! Even when we cook for our Arabia pop-up restaurant, everybody leaves with doggy bags so they can enjoy the leftovers the next day. We provide them for the reactions alone. And although we've adapted things here, be aware that our quantities for four to six people can often please five to eight people. There is a famous Moroccan saying that when you divide a dish between two plates, it's enough for two; if you serve the dish in a large bowl to share, then the same amount of food can feed ten. If you are making several dishes, be aware of the quantities: half the amount will suffice. Except when, just like us, you want to make everyone around you happy. In that case make enough or too much, allow everyone to take home containers, and become immortal. You can eat almost all dishes with bread: from flatbread to Turkish or Moroccan bread, or simply your own homemade bread. Bread is holy in the Arab world. No bread, no life.

Lots of food at lunch

We love sumptuous lunches. You can sample many dishes, relax, and still have enough time to digest all that food. A Saturday or Sunday Arabia lunch is perfect for inviting friends and family (ideally people who don't know each other, a mix of young and old!), to catch up, to quietly enjoy lots of food, and to put conversation skills to good use.

Simple recipes

It's commonly believed that Arabic cuisine is very complex and uses many ingredients in one recipe, but most dishes actually are very simple and not expensive to prepare. And while the flavors are very rich (even more so because you often eat several dishes at the same time), almost all recipes are quite approachable for even the novice cook. The most important thing is to taste, taste, taste! We always use many spices and herbs, and a lot of olive oil and lemon juice. Don't be afraid—just sample and then season to taste. What if you lack a certain ingredient? It's not the end of the world; you can do it without it, or replace the ingredient with something else. No cilantro? Use parsley. No bulgur? Use small pasta. No almonds? Use hazelnuts or walnuts. You might come up with an interesting variation. We love to forget an ingredient: It forces us to improvise and that's when delicious things start to happen! This cuisine also follows the seasons: When there are quinces available, you'll prepare them in various ways. The same goes for fava beans, artichokes, and other seasonal fruits and vegetables.

Kitchen utensils

A good chopping board and a sharp chef's knife are indispensable for all your cutting and slicing. A large, sturdy mortar and pestle is also good to have: You'll use it to grind herbs, nuts, and spices. Of course, you can also do this with a hand blender or simply by chopping and mincing, but once you've discovered the mortar and pestle you won't want to use anything else. It's an ideal way to blow off steam! A food processor or hand blender is indispensable for hummus and most soups. If you want to steam your couscous and if you believe you'll make many tajine dishes, it's worth the effort to buy a real couscoussière (a steamer and pan in two parts) and an earthenware tajine (a pot consisting of a round base and a funnel-shaped cover). Forget about the modern versions in fancy cookware stores; the old-fashioned Moroccan variety found in Middle Eastern shops works best. You can also use a Dutch oven. We are addicted to the Microplane grater for grating citrus zest as well as ginger, garlic, and so on. A mandoline slicer is nice to have for shaving vegetables in very thin slices; if you don't have one, simply use a cheese slicer or a sharp knife.

Ingredients and culinary pantry

We have organized the recipes in this book according to their most important ingredients: In each chapter, we cover one type of ingredient, such as couscous, bulgur, or orange

blossom water. We explain what it is, how delicious it tastes, how to use it, and where you can buy it. When you buy an ingredient from every chapter in the book you'll have created your own basic Arabic culinary pantry, and you'll be able to make do for most recipes by combining with fresh vegetables and spices, fish, and meat. Look for Moroccan, Turkish, and Middle Eastern sources in the back of the book (page 278).

How to use our recipes

Parsley is always flat-leaf parsley. Try to purchase large bunches, the way you would buy them in a Turkish or Moroccan store.

fish is always of the best quality, in season, and as sustainable as possible. Ask your fishmonger what's good.

We list salt and pepper only in the recipe directions, not among the ingredients, because cooking without salt and pepper is impossible. It's best if you have both fine and coarse salt on hand, and ideally also salt flakes, such as Maldon sea salt. We use spices generously, and you might want to start with less and add more to suit your own personal taste.

A basic Arabian glossary

There are a couple words that summarize Arabic cuisine wonderfully. The dishes are always a feast for the eyes, and in fact for all your senses. They are true aromatic explosions in your mouth and they stimulate body and soul. We say *bismilla* and *sahtein*.

Yalla! Get to work!

Bismilla and **sahtein** bon appetit and santé (in Moroccan and Lebanese)

Meska horra mastic, a resin (sometimes called Arabic gum) used across the Middle East for everything from smoked meats to desserts.

Khobz bread

Mai water

Mazahar orange blossom water

Ma'ward rose water

> *All we eat has been alive*
> *The act of love makes life*
> *So food—is life—is love*
> *Make love—eat life*
> **Søren Wiuff**

(Søren is the vegetable supplier to Noma, Rene Redzepi's famous three-star restaurant in Copenhagen.)

Olive oil is usually a grassy, fruity extra virgin oil for salads and to season dishes. We use a mild olive oil for baking and, in some dishes, we use a specific olive oil, like a rustic Moroccan oil.

We prefer to use organic citrus fruit because we like to eat the skin as well.

All vegetables are washed, peeled, or cleaned.
In our recipes, 1 clove of garlic means 1 peeled clove of garlic and 1 onion means 1 peeled onion. Nuts are always skinned, unless stated otherwise, and everything is fresh, if possible. We like to buy organic chicken and meat. Our

• CONTENTS •

THE TREE
of LIFE!

Every dish deserves its own olive oil.
Hummus and labneh like a fruity green
olive oil, for example a Greek or Italian
one from Puglia. Rustic Middle Eastern
dishes prefer a flavorful nabali or rumi
olive oil. And for some specific
Moroccan peasant dishes we choose a
potent rustic olive oil from Ouazzane,
a town in northern Morocco.

Bitter with a bite or savory salty

Middle Eastern olives are very different from
Moroccan olives; they are usually more bitter.
They are green, cracked nabali, souri, or baladi
olives, and they're divine. You can find them in
Middle Eastern groceries. We like to eat them with our
meals—breakfast, lunch, and mezze. The black Turkish
breakfast olives (that's what they are called!) are worthy
of their name. We love to eat Moroccan olives, whether
the salty, black, wrinkled olives, the pickled green olives
with red-hot pepper and preserved lemon, or the purple
lemon olives, for breakfast or lunch, with fresh bread
on the side. It's also delicious to pit black Moroccan
olives and toss them in a dish. We like to eat small
Spanish and Italian olives, like arbequina and
taggiasca, in between meals or in dishes.

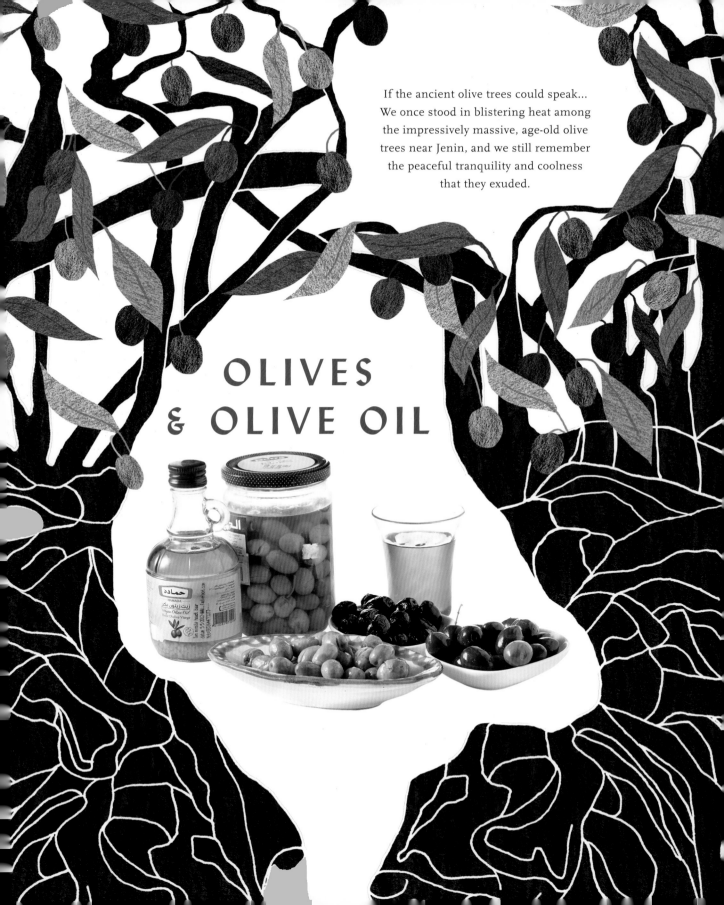

If the ancient olive trees could speak...
We once stood in blistering heat among
the impressively massive, age-old olive
trees near Jenin, and we still remember
the peaceful tranquility and coolness
that they exuded.

OLIVES
& OLIVE OIL

When we were in Puglia, Italy, it struck us how similar the food was to dishes we knew from the Middle East: the way people eat green, slightly bitter vegetables, and also the hummus-like mixtures, the white cheese, and the cookies and other sweets—it was just like Lebanon! This is a wonderful dish to celebrate the fruity green olive oil from Puglia, which tastes like green tomato and artichoke.

Chicory from Puglia

With chickpea puree

SERVES 4

9 ounces (250 g) dried chickpeas (soaked overnight, see page 82)

2 cloves garlic

Mild olive oil

6 anchovy fillets (ideally preserved in salt, otherwise in olive oil)

1 peperoncino or Aleppo pepper (see page 44)

1 head chicory

Fruity green olive oil

- Cover the chickpeas with water and boil until tender, about 45 minutes.
- Finely slice the garlic and sauté in a large sauté pan with a generous splash of mild olive oil. Add the anchovies and some chopped pepperoncino and allow the fish to melt in, about 10 minutes. Separate the chicory leaves and chop coarsely. Add the chicory to the sauté pan, stirring occasionally, until tender, about 10 minutes. Season with some salt, but be careful: the anchovies are also salty.
- Puree half of the chickpeas with a dash of water and some salt, then stir in the remaining chickpeas. Serve the chickpea puree with the chicory; if you wish you also can serve with Oven-Dried Olives (page 12). Drizzle everything generously with fruity green olive oil, preferably from Puglia.

We once secretly picked olives in Puglia. We put as many as we could carry in a plastic bag. At home we pickled them and dried them in the oven. We kept at it with "regular" black, wrinkled olives and kalamata olives, inspired by oven-dried olives from the country estate and organic farm La Vialla in Tuscany. When they dry olives in large quantities, the aroma fills the countryside.

Oven-Dried Olives

With garlic, bay leaf, and orange

SERVES 4 TO 6

1¼ cups (200 g) black Moroccan wrinkled olives

1¼ cups (200 g) pink kalamata olives

3 cloves garlic

Zest of 1 orange

4 fresh bay leaves

3 cups (720 ml) olive oil

- Preheat the oven to 122°F (50°C). Dab the olives dry with a paper towel. Chop the garlic into thin slices (if present, remove the green kernel). With a zester, slice thin strips of the orange peel from the orange. Tear the bay leaves into small pieces.
- Combine the olives, garlic, orange zest, and bay leaves, and spread them out over a large baking sheet. Let the mixture dry in the oven for about 8 hours. Transfer to a lidded jar and cover with the olive oil. Store the olives in the pantry or keep them on the counter. The olive oil will absorb the flavors of the olives and will be delicious as a base for a dressing or drizzled over dishes.

This classic soup is a staple of Moroccan cuisine and therefore couldn't be absent from this book. But we offer our own version, with cumin, celery oil, and small poached quail eggs. Don't be put off by the long list of ingredients—the preparation is very simple.

Harira

With cumin, celery oil, and poached quail eggs

SERVES 6 TO 8

1 (14-ounce / 400-g) can peeled tomatoes

1 (6-ounce / 170-g) can tomato paste

3 onions, coarsely chopped

1 clove garlic, coarsely chopped

¾-inch (2-cm) piece ginger, peeled

1 bunch celery leaves (keep a few sprigs separate)

1 bunch flat-leaf parsley

1 bunch cilantro

4 tablespoons (36 g) Ras el Hanout (page 170)

4 tablespoons (36 g) cinnamon

2 tablespoons ground cumin

1 tablespoon fenugreek

2 tablespoons ground ginger

Mild olive oil

10½ ounces (300 g) chickpeas (soaked overnight, see page 82)

1 small butternut squash

5¼ ounces (150 g) brown lentils (see page 82)

Scant ½ cup (50 g) all-purpose flour

12 quail eggs

Vinegar, for poaching, optional

Fruity green olive oil

1 tablespoon cumin seeds

- Put the peeled tomatoes, tomato paste, onions, garlic, ginger, celery, parsley, cilantro, ras el hanout, cinnamon, cumin, fenugreek, and ginger in a large soup pot, add 4½ cups (1 L) water and a generous splash of mild olive oil, and puree with a hand blender until smooth. Add the soaked chickpeas and bring to a boil. Let the soup boil gently for about 30 minutes.
- Meanwhile, peel the squash, remove the seeds, and chop in small chunks. Add the squash cubes and lentils to the soup and gently boil for another 30 minutes, or until the chickpeas are tender. Mix the flour with ¾ cup (180 ml) water, stir in the soup, and let simmer for a few minutes.
- Meanwhile, poach the quail eggs. In a wide, shallow pan, bring water to a boil and add a dash of vinegar, if desired. Break each egg in its own cup. Create a whirl in the water with a spoon and let the eggs slide in, three at a time at most. Poach until softly set, about 3 minutes. Spoon the eggs out of the water with a skimmer and let them drain on a plate.
- With a hand blender, puree the remaining sprigs of celery with the fruity green olive oil, cumin seeds, and 1 teaspoon salt flakes.
- Divide the soup into large bowls, slide a few poached eggs in each bowl, and drizzle with the cumin-celery oil. This soup is an elegant starter, but with some Moroccan bread it's also delicious as a main course. It can be the perfect way to break the fast during Ramadan.

According to oral tradition, it used to be possible to walk from Libya to Morocco under the shade of olive trees.

The idea for this recipe came from the walnut cake made by Nadia's mother, Fadila, and the carob cake made by the restaurant Tawlet in Beirut. The sweet ras el hanout makes it wonderfully fragrant and the olive oil creates a soft, smooth texture. Carob powder is made from the pods of the carob tree. This tree is found everywhere in Mediterranean countries and the powder is used as a sweet paste. The taste is vaguely reminiscent of cacao. Look for carob molasses in Middle Eastern groceries or order it online.

Olive Oil Cake

With carob, pine nuts, and sweet ras el hanout

SERVES 4 TO 6

8 ounces (250 g) pine nuts

6 large eggs

¾ cup (180 ml) carob molasses, or date syrup

¾ cup (180 ml) fruity green olive oil, plus some extra for greasing the pan

2 cups (250 g) all-purpose flour, sifted, plus some extra for dusting the pan

1 tablespoon baking powder

2 tablespoons sweet ras el hanout (see page 170)

Dried rose petals

OPTIONAL

3 tablespoons light brown sugar

- Preheat the oven to 325°F (165°C). Oil and flour a 10-inch (25-cm) cake pan, preferably springform. Finely grind the pine nuts. With a hand blender or whisk, beat the eggs with the carob molasses and the oil (if you have a sweet tooth, you can add the light brown sugar) until thick and creamy, about 10 minutes. With a whisk, beat in the pine nuts. Then bit by bit, sift in the flour, the baking powder and the sweet ras el hanout (if there are any large bits of spice left in the sieve, discard them); whip it as quickly as possible into the egg mixture.

- Pour the batter into the prepared pan. Bake the cake for 45 to 50 minutes in the middle of the oven, until a toothpick or cake tester inserted in the middle comes out clean and dry.

- Let the cake cool in the pan for a few minutes, then remove to a cake rack or plate and let cool completely. Before serving, sprinkle with some sweet ras el hanout and dried rose petals. Lovely with Arabic or Turkish coffee.

This cauliflower couscous was once concocted in the city of Batroun, Lebanon, from the only ingredients on hand: cauliflower, delicious Batrouni lemons, and the famous long Lebanese pine nuts. Cauliflower couscous was once featured in *delicious* magazine, and we have given it a new twist because we just couldn't resist. This couscous has lots of parsley and orange zest.

Green Cauliflower Couscous

With citrus zest and pine nuts

SERVES 4 TO 6

1 large cauliflower

2 bunches flat-leaf parsley

1 lemon

1 orange

3¼ ounces (75 g) pine nuts

Mild olive oil

Fruity green olive oil

- Quarter the cauliflower and grate the chunks with a fine grater into a fine couscous-like texture. Chop the parsley very fine. Grate the lemon and orange zest, then squeeze the lemon and orange for their juice; set the juice aside. Mix the chopped parsley and grated citrus zest with the cauliflower couscous.

- In a small frying pan, sauté the pine nuts in a small amount of mild olive oil until golden brown. Drain the nuts on a paper towel and chop them once they've cooled.

- Season the cauliflower with the lemon and orange juice, salt, and plenty of fruity green olive oil. Mix in the pine nuts just before serving.

Rice for the poor

Bulgur was long considered inferior to rice in the Middle East. In Lebanon and Syria, some people swear by mujaddara (a dish made with lentils and served with fried onion on top) with bulgur, while others eat it with rice. It differs from village to village but everybody keeps strictly to their own rule. Georgina Al Bayeh, a chef from the restaurant Tawlet (located at the Beirut farmer's market Souk el Tayeb), with whom we cook regularly, is from Kfardebian, in the north of Lebanon. She often makes her mujaddara with bulgur. "That's the way I was taught in the village where I grew up, although I actually prefer rice." But Georgina, why don't you make it with rice, we suggest. "No, I can't," she says, shaking her head. "Here we make it with bulgur."

All sorts of bulgur

Bulgur comes in three varieties: fine, medium-fine, and coarse, in both a "white" and a whole-wheat version. What is bulgur, actually? It's a cracked wheat that is steamed (or precooked) and then dried. Therefore you never have to cook bulgur for very long and you can even use fine bulgur raw in salads, as in the famous Lebanese-Syrian tabouleh and the Turkish kisir salad. To soften it you can sprinkle the raw fine bulgur with some water or lemon juice, but it's not truly neccessary because the crunchiness adds to the taste. Fine bulgur is also used in köfte: ground beef or lentils mixed with bulgur. Turkish cig köfte contains only bulgur mixed with tomato-paprika paste and fresh herbs. Kibbeh or kubbeh, içli köfte, or oruk (different names for the same dish) is ground beef mixed with bulgur, kneaded like a dough, and then molded into nice egg-shaped little balls stuffed with ground meat, onion, and pine nuts. These are deep-fried until crunchy. You can also create patties, using them almost like a flatbread. In Iraq, they put very thin layers of meat between the patties. Delicious!

Medium-fine and coarse bulgur is
used for pilafs and soups. We also find bulgur
delicious as a filler in vegetable salads.
Freekeh has a special, lightly smoked, nutty
taste that is also delicious in pilafs and soups.

BULGUR & FREEKEH

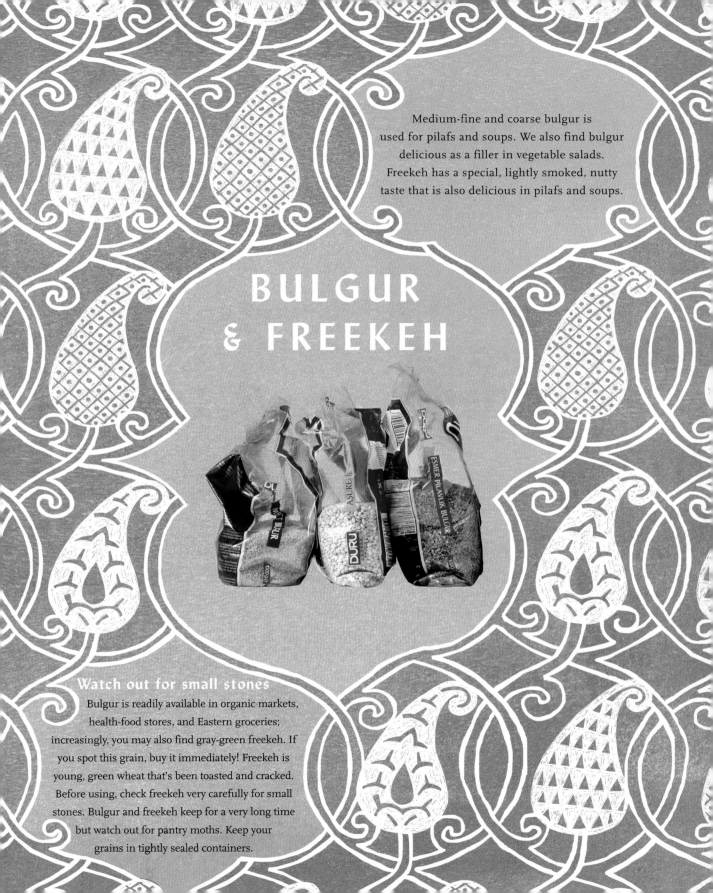

Watch out for small stones

Bulgur is readily available in organic markets,
health-food stores, and Eastern groceries;
increasingly, you may also find gray-green freekeh. If
you spot this grain, buy it immediately! Freekeh is
young, green wheat that's been toasted and cracked.
Before using, check freekeh very carefully for small
stones. Bulgur and freekeh keep for a very long time
but watch out for pantry moths. Keep your
grains in tightly sealed containers.

Wheat berries also make a terrific base for salads, although they are a little less familiar than bulgur, rice, or pasta. This recipe is actually a collection of our favorite ingredients: orange juice dressing, fennel seed, hazelnuts, and artichokes. This salad is lovely as an entree, but also delicious for an Arabia buffet. Look for wheat berries and frozen artichoke bottoms in upscale food markets or Middle Eastern groceries.

Wheat Salad

With caramelized artichokes, fennel seed, and beet tops

SERVES 6 TO 8

2 cups (300 g) wheat berries

2 cups (480 ml) freshly squeezed orange juice

1 (16-ounce / 450-g) bag frozen artichoke bottoms

4 red onions

4 cloves garlic

Mild olive oil

2 tablespoons fennel seed

¾ cup (75 g) hazelnuts

Lemon juice

5 ounces (125 g) young beet tops, chard, or baby Swiss chard

3 ounces (75 g) arugula

- In a pot filled with ample salted water, boil the wheat berries for about 1 hour, making sure they are still al dente. Drain and rinse with cold water.
- Bring the orange juice to a boil in a small saucepan and allow to reduce to a thick syrup over low heat. Watch carefully: The juice can burn easily! Set aside to cool.
- Thaw the artichoke bottoms and quarter them. Cut the onions in wedges. Slice the garlic. Heat a thick layer of mild olive oil in a deep frying pan and sauté the onions and artichokes over medium heat for about 5 minutes. Add the garlic, fennel seed, and salt to taste and allow to caramelize for about 1 hour over very low heat. Turn off the heat and let the mixture cool in the oil.
- Roast the hazelnuts until golden brown in a hot, dry sauté pan. Remove to a plate to cool. Drain any remaining oil from the caramelized vegetables and use it to make a dressing with the condensed juice, salt, pepper, and lemon juice to taste.
- Before serving, combine the wheat berries with the caramelized vegetables, the hazelnuts, beet tops, and arugula. Mix in the dressing.

Kibbeh batata (potato kibbeh) is another classic from Lebanese cuisine in which potatoes are combined with bulgur mixed with sabaa baharat (7-spices). Regular kibbeh is made from ground lamb mixed with bulgur. This is our funky version with orange and lemon zest, which was jubilantly received in Beirut. Another Arabia buffet favorite.

Potato Kibbeh

With orange and lemon zest

SERVES 6 TO 8

1 pound (500 g) large Yukon gold potatoes

1 bunch scallions

¾ cup (125 g) fine bulgur (see page 22)

Grated zest of ½ orange

Grated zest of 1 lemon

Fruity green olive oil

Aleppo pepper (see page 44)

- In a large pot of richly salted water, boil the potatoes in their skins for 30 minutes, or until tender. Finely slice the scallions and set aside. Let the potatoes cool, then peel and mash them until smooth. Press the potatoes through a fine-mesh sieve if any lumps remain.
- With your hands, knead the bulgur, three-quarters of the scallions, the citrus zest, and a dash of water into the potatoes. Season with some extra salt and add, if you wish, an extra dash of water: The kibbeh should be smooth, but not a puree. With wet hands, spread the mixture into a ½-inch (1-cm) deep plate, and smooth the surface. With the back of a knife you can carve a kibbeh pattern (see picture) or make your own pattern.
- Drizzle the kibbeh generously with olive oil and sprinkle the rest of the scallions and the Aleppo pepper on top.

The bulgar salad is earthy, tangy, and fresh and an ideal salad for a "vitamin boost." You don't really need anything else. This is another perfect buffet dish (for buffet ideas see page 274).

Bulgur Salad

With pomegranate molasses, roasted squash, and pistachio

SERVES 6 TO 8

2 cups (300 g) whole-wheat bulgur (see page 22)

Lemon juice

Fruity green olive oil

1 small butternut squash

Mild olive oil

1 pomegranate

1 bunch scallions

1 bunch flat-leaf parsley

¾ cup (75 g) shelled pistachio nuts

Pomegranate molasses (see page 138)

- Combine the bulgur with a few tablespoons of lemon juice and a generous splash of fruity green olive oil. Preheat the oven to 400°F (200°C).
- Halve the squash, remove the seeds, and cut in thin slices. Lay the slices in a baking tray, sprinkle with salt, drizzle with some mild olive oil, and roast for 10 minutes, or until golden brown.
- Meanwhile, peel the pomegranate: Cut off the crown and crack the pomegranate open with your thumbs. Peel out the arils and make sure the white pith doesn't come along. Finely chop the scallions and the parsley. Roast the pistachio nuts until golden brown in the hot oven; let them cool and then chop coarsely.
- Mix the bulgur with the squash, pomegranate arils, scallions, parsley, and pistachio nuts and season well with a generous amount of pomegranate molasses, some lemon juice, olive oil, and salt.

Freekeh is green, unripe wheat that is usually lightly smoked: The bunches of wheat are set on fire, and afterward the black, scorched grains are rubbed loose and cleaned. *Freek* is Arabic for "rubbing." In the Middle East, freekeh is used for pilafs and soups. This rustic peasant soup is ideal for fall and winter.

Hearty Freekeh Soup

With chickpeas and lamb

SERVES 4 TO 6

2 onions

1 clove garlic

Mild olive oil

9 ounces (250 g) lamb shoulder, boneless

½ teaspoon allspice

1 cinnamon stick

1½ cups (250 g) freekeh (see page 22)

1 cup (200 g) chickpeas (soaked overnight, see page 82)

Fruity green olive oil

2 tablespoons finely chopped flat-leaf parsley

- Finely chop the onions and garlic. Heat a generous splash of olive oil in a large pan and sauté the onions and garlic for about 10 minutes on low heat. Cube the meat and add it, along with the allspice and the cinnamon stick. Then add the freekeh and the chickpeas, stir thoroughly, turn up the heat, and add 4½ cups (1 L) water and salt.
- Simmer the soup over low heat for about 40 minutes and add some extra water if needed (it should remain a very thick soup). Season well.
- Serve the soup in bowls with some fruity green olive oil drizzled in and sprinkle with parsley.

Make sure to season this salad well with olive oil, lemon juice, and salt just before serving. The large bulgur grains absorb a lot of the seasonings, which can make the salad taste bland, so taste it often while you're making it. Turkish nomad cheese (tulum) is a soft goat cheese. You can keep it in a glass jar in the fridge for a long time; it's ideal to have on hand as part of your Arabia pantry.

Bulgur Salad

With fava beans, dill, and paprika herb paste

SERVES 8 TO 10

3 cups (500 g) medium-fine bulgur (see page 22)

Juice from 2 lemons

2 bunches dill

3 bunches flat-leaf parsley

Handful of mint leaves

1 bunch scallions

8 ounces (250 g) dry Turkish nomad cheese (tulum, see page 126)

1 clove garlic, minced

1 (6-ounce / 170-g) can tomato paste

4 tablespoons (60 g) Turkish paprika paste (see page 44)

¾ cup (180 ml) fruity green olive oil

3 cups (350 g) fava beans (freshly shelled or frozen)

- Sprinkle the bulgur with the lemon juice. Finely chop the dill, parsley, mint leaves, and scallions.
- Combine the nomad cheese with 2 tablespoons of the dill, 2 tablespoons of the mint, the garlic, tomato paste, paprika paste, and olive oil. Season with salt and fold the herb-cheese mixture into the bulgur.
- Boil the beans for 5 minutes and let them drain, cooling them under running water. Add these to the bulgur as well and stir in the remaining dill, parsley, and scallions. Taste and season right before serving with olive oil, lemon juice, and salt as needed.

Jerusalem-Style Preserved Lemons

Slice 4 lemons. In a clean jar that's been scalded in hot water, alternate layers of a few lemon slices with a generous sprinkling of coarse sea salt and Aleppo pepper, or red pepper flakes. The jar should be filled up completely, with the lemons tightly packed in salt. Put on the lid and store the jar in a dark, cool space for a couple of weeks before using. They are wonderful when finely sliced atop a bowl of hummus.

Metamorphosis

When brined, fresh, zesty lemons undergo a true metamorphosis. The texture of the zest changes: It becomes soft. The taste ripens and becomes salty, with a hint of flowery citrus notes. The pulp, however, turns salty-bitter and isn't tasty at all. Don't use it. Just remove it with a knife and use only the beautiful, smooth zest. Finely mince or dice it to use in salads, sauces, and dressings, or in stews like tajines.

It's easy to make preserved lemons yourself. You can also buy them—even easier, but less delicious. They're sold in plastic containers, but you can often find them at the olive bar of your Middle Eastern grocery as well (these are usually better). Avoid the ones that come in glass jars, however; they tend to have a funny taste.

Homemade preserved lemons

Here is the classic method for making preserved lemons: Quarter 4 lemons but don't cut through all the way—leave the parts connected. Sprinkle each lemon with a full spoon of coarse sea salt. Pack the lemons to the top of a clean jar that's been scalded in hot water. Keep in a cool, dark place and, after some liquid has accumulated, add a generous splash of orange blossom water. Leave for another few weeks before using.

Classic dishes made with preserved lemons are chicken tajine with green olives; lukewarm Moroccan carrot salad with cumin, cilantro, and harissa; and green or light purple olives with preserved lemons.

Bergamot oranges

You may sometimes be able to find bergamot oranges from Calabria. This member of the citrus family has an instantly recognizable aroma (you know it from Earl Grey tea, which gets its flavor from bergamot citrus oil). These bergamot oranges are also great for making delicious confits.

PRESERVED LEMONS

From Marrakech to Jeruselem

We always liked to think of preserved lemons as typically Moroccan. But they are prevalent in Jeruselem as well, having made their way there via Moroccan Jews. This is why a lot of Moroccan dishes, like couscous and salty preserved lemons, are popular there. Food travels, unfettered by borders.

These grilled potatoes are a big hit among our friends. We learned how to make them when visiting family homes in Lebanon, where our hosts prepared them on heating stoves that doubled as ovens and cookers, and at Maguy's fish restaurant in the city of Batroun, where they make them on a charcoal grill. It's very simple: Thinly slice the potatoes and generously sprinkle them with salt. Then grill or bake them in a dry skillet or on an outdoor grill. No need to precook them. The result is a nicely charred potato that hasn't lost its crunch, which is delicious. The salsa verde with preserved lemon simply invited itself to the menu!

Grilled Potatoes
With salsa verde and preserved lemon

SERVES 8 TO 10

6 large Yukon gold potatoes

1 bunch flat-leaf parsley

1 bunch basil

½ bunch mint

1 bunch cilantro

½ preserved lemon (see page 34)

Grated zest of 1 lemon

1 clove garlic

¾ cup (180 ml) fruity green olive oil

• Slice the unpeeled potatoes lengthwise. Heat a dry skillet and grill the potato slices for a few minutes on either side, until they get brown blisters. Don't cook them all the way; they should still be a bit crispy.

• Pick the herbs. Remove the pulp from the preserved lemon and cut the peel into fine slices. Using a hand blender, mash the herbs, the preserved lemon, the lemon zest, garlic, and olive oil and season with salt. Serve the potatoes with the salsa verde.

Moghrabieh comes from the word "Maghreb." This Middle Eastern answer to couscous is basically a ball-shaped pasta, and here we've made a type of risotto with it. The moghrabieh is cooked in a delicious sauce that we seasoned with cinnamon and allspice, typical Middle Eastern seasonings. The fishcakes with preserved lemon and harissa have more of a Maghreb origin, but once on the plate, they get along nicely. If you can't find moghrabieh in a Middle Eastern grocery, replace it with Turkish barley pasta or Italian *fregola* from Sardinia, which you can find in most Italian delis.

Moghrabieh

And fishcakes with preserved lemon and harissa

SERVES 4

5 small vine-ripened tomatoes

2 small sweet onions

Mild olive oil

1 tablespoon cinnamon

½ tablespoon allspice

5 vine-ripened tomatoes

1¾ cups (350 g) moghrabieh (Lebanese couscous)

½ preserved lemon (see page 34)

14 ounces (400 g) halibut, striped bass, or other firm white fish

1 bunch flat-leaf parsley, chopped

1 clove garlic, chopped

2 tablespoons harissa (see page 44)

• Bring a large pot of water to boil. Using a sharp knife, slice a shallow X into the bottom of each tomatoes and submerge them in the boiling water for about 1 minute. Peel the skin off the tomatoes and dice them. Mince the onions. In a large frying pan, heat a generous amount of olive oil over medium heat and sauté the onions with the cinnamon and allspice for about 10 minutes, stirring frequently and lowering the heat to keep them from burning. Add the tomatoes and mix in the moghrabieh as well. Add 4½ cups (1 L) water and about ½ teaspoon salt. Cook the pasta over low heat for about 30 minutes, stirring frequently toward the end, until it is thick and creamy like risotto. (Add some water if the pasta is cooking dry.) Season with salt if needed.

• Remove the pulp from the preserved lemon and slice the peel into thin strips. In a food processor, puree the fish with the preserved lemon, parsley, garlic, and harissa. Season with a pinch of salt. Shape the fish mixture into small, flat cakes (this is best done with wet hands). Heat some oil in a skillet (nonstick works best for these delicate patties) and fry the fish cakes until golden brown on both sides and cooked through, about 3 minutes per side. Serve over the moghrabieh.

It seems odd to have a wintry salad, but that's really what this dish is: a mix of pilaf and salad, full of flavor and contrast. Turnips are available throughout the year, but in the wintertime they're usually a bit larger.

Wintry Bulgur Salad

With turnips, preserved lemon, and pomegranate-walnut dressing

SERVES 4 TO 6

5 turnips

2 tablespoons butter

½ preserved lemon (see page 34)

¾ cup (75 g) walnuts

¾ cup (180 ml) pomegranate molasses (see page 138)

Grated zest and juice of 1 orange

Fruity green olive oil

1½ cups (350 g) cooked whole-wheat bulgur (page 22)

1 bunch flat-leaf parsley

5 sprigs oregano

Handful of black Spanish, Italian, or Moroccan olives

- Clean and quarter the turnips. In a large sauté pan, melt the butter over low heat and slowly cook the turnips for 30 minutes, or until tender when pierced with a fork. Season with some salt.

- Remove the pulp from the preserved lemon and slice the peel into thin strips. Place the walnuts in a deep bowl with the pomegranate molasses and orange juice and puree with a hand blender. Season with a generous splash of olive oil and some salt. Mix the dressing into the cooked bulgur.

- Finely chop the parsley and pick the oregano. Combine the turnips, preserved lemon, orange zest, parsley, and oregano with the bulgur. Taste and season with some salt, if needed. Sprinkle the olives over the finished dish.

Our version of the famous Moroccan fava bean salad is so wonderful you will simply devour it—especially early in the fava bean season, when the beans are small and very tender. We're addicted to coriander seed (see page 70) and use it here to replace the traditional cumin.

Fava Bean Salad

With almonds and preserved lemon

SERVES 4 TO 6

2½ pounds (1 kg) fresh fava beans

Mild olive oil

1¼ cups (150 g) blanched almonds

1 preserved lemon

2 tablespoons coriander seed

Fruity green olive oil

- Clean and shell half of the beans. Clean the other half, but don't shell them: Trim any edges and hard grains, then cut them—legume and all—into large chunks. Steam or cook the unshelled beans until tender, about 30 minutes; add the shelled beans after 10 minutes. Once the beans are tender, thoroughly drain them.

- In a deep sauté pan, heat a good amount of mild olive oil and deep-fry the almonds until they're golden brown. Chop coarsely. Remove the pulp from the preserved lemon and thinly slice the peel. Coarsely crush the coriander seed. Mix the beans with the nuts, lemon peel, and coriander and season with the fruity green oil and some salt.

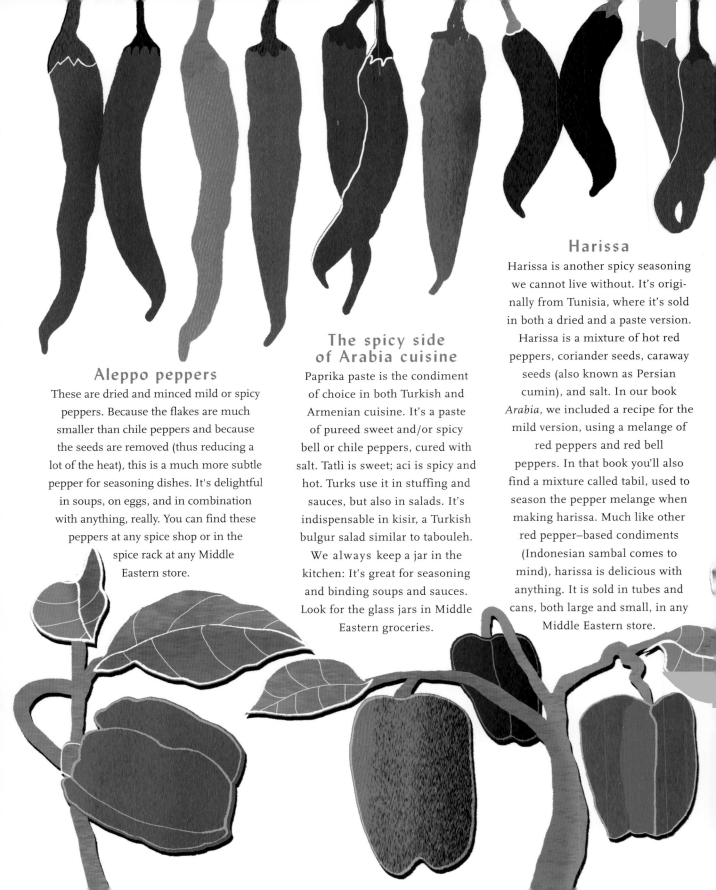

Aleppo peppers

These are dried and minced mild or spicy peppers. Because the flakes are much smaller than chile peppers and because the seeds are removed (thus reducing a lot of the heat), this is a much more subtle pepper for seasoning dishes. It's delightful in soups, on eggs, and in combination with anything, really. You can find these peppers at any spice shop or in the spice rack at any Middle Eastern store.

The spicy side of Arabia cuisine

Paprika paste is the condiment of choice in both Turkish and Armenian cuisine. It's a paste of pureed sweet and/or spicy bell or chile peppers, cured with salt. Tatli is sweet; aci is spicy and hot. Turks use it in stuffing and sauces, but also in salads. It's indispensable in kisir, a Turkish bulgur salad similar to tabouleh.

We always keep a jar in the kitchen: It's great for seasoning and binding soups and sauces. Look for the glass jars in Middle Eastern groceries.

Harissa

Harissa is another spicy seasoning we cannot live without. It's originally from Tunisia, where it's sold in both a dried and a paste version. Harissa is a mixture of hot red peppers, coriander seeds, caraway seeds (also known as Persian cumin), and salt. In our book *Arabia,* we included a recipe for the mild version, using a melange of red peppers and red bell peppers. In that book you'll also find a mixture called tabil, used to season the pepper melange when making harissa. Much like other red pepper–based condiments (Indonesian sambal comes to mind), harissa is delicious with anything. It is sold in tubes and cans, both large and small, in any Middle Eastern store.

PAPRIKA PASTE, HARISSA
& ALEPPO PEPPER

We love the powerful, almost meatlike taste of savoy cabbage, especially with the added fiery punch of some harissa and garlic. This is a heavenly side dish for roasted lamb chops and some good bread.

Stir-Fried Savoy Cabbage

With harissa and garlic

SERVES 4

1 small head savoy or green cabbage

2 cloves garlic

Mild olive oil

2 tablespoons harissa (page 44)

Fruity green olive oil

• Slice the cabbage into long strips. Grate the garlic. In a large sauté pan, heat a good amount of mild olive oil and fry the garlic and the harissa for about 2 minutes.
• Add the cabbage and stir-fry for about 10 minutes. Add a splash of water, if necessary. Taste and season with some salt, if needed. Drizzle with fruity green olive oil.

We use Arabic ingredients in this Spanish fish soup. We put Turkish paprika paste and coriander seeds in the Catalan *picada*: a paste of crushed hazelnuts or almonds, with garlic and *pimentón*. It's a recipe with deep Arabic roots, which we learned from the Catalan *abuelas* (grandmothers). To the *sofregit*, a traditional steamed Catalan tomato-based sauce, we added some Turkish paprika paste. If you can't find cockles, use small, hard-shell clams instead; cod or haddock is a good substitute for the hake fish.

Fish Soup

With sofregit, paprika paste, and garlic picada

SERVES 4 TO 6

1¼ pound common cockles (500 g)

2 onions

Mild olive oil

4 tablespoons (60 g) Turkish paprika paste (see page 44)

2 tablespoons tomato paste

Zest of 1 lemon, sliced (without the white pith)

2 tablespoons coriander seed, divided

1 bunch flat-leaf parsley, stems and leaves separated

14 ounces (400 g) hake tail fillet, in wedges

1 cup (100 g) almonds

1 clove garlic

Fruity green olive oil

- Place the cockles in a bowl of cold water. Slice the onions and cut the rings in half. In a large, deep sauté pan, heat a good amount of mild olive oil and sauté the onions for about 5 minutes. Add the paprika paste and tomato paste and cook on low heat for about 10 minutes. Add the sliced lemon zest, 1 tablespoon of the coriander seed, the stems of the parsley, some salt, and 4½ cups (1 L) water. Let the soup simmer for about 20 minutes over low heat. Add the fish and simmer for 10 minutes, or until the fish is tender. Rinse the cockles with cold water, and add them to the soup 5 minutes after the fish.
- Crush together the almonds, garlic, parsley leaves, the remaining coriander seed, some salt, and a splash of the fruity green olive oil to make a *picada* (paste). Stir the picada into the soup and serve.

In a little fish restaurant on the beach of Latakia in Syria, we once ate a mouthwatering *samak harra* (spicy fish). We serve our version with a nutty, creamy tahini sauce. To the marinade we added some fresh lemon zest. The combination of spicy and nutty flavors is finger-licking good! For connoisseurs: This samak harra can be eaten with your hands. We used tub gurnard for this recipe, which is a North Atlantic fish. A sea bream or a whole sea bass is a good substitute.

Samak Harra

With harissa, Aleppo pepper, and tahini sauce

SERVES 2 TO 3

2 cloves garlic

4 tablespoons (60 g) harissa (see page 44)

2 tablespoons Aleppo pepper (see page 44)

Grated zest of 1 lemon

Mild olive oil

1 sizable (up to 5-pound / 2-kg) tub gurnard

2 tablespoons tahini (see page 58)

Sumac, to taste

- Preheat the oven to 375°F (190°C). Grate the garlic and, in a small bowl, combine it with the harissa, Aleppo pepper, lemon zest, and a little olive oil; season with salt. Rub the fish with this mixture and place it in an ovenproof baking dish. Depending on its size, roast the fish for 15 to 35 minutes, until the fish flakes easily when prodded with a knife near the backbone.
- In a small bowl, whisk the tahini together with enough hot water to make a smooth sauce. Season with sumac and salt to taste.
- Generously ladle the tahini sauce over the fish (the rest can be served in a little side bowl) and serve.

In the Middle East, popular wisdom has it that a wife should prepare spicy food for her husband because bland food bespeaks love without passion.

An everyday comfort-food stew that is full of flavor, thanks to the combination of spicy harissa, hot sausages, and sweet potato. And it takes only a minute!

Harissa Stew

With merguez and sweet potato

SERVES 2

2 large sweet potatoes

1 clove garlic

1 onion

Mild olive oil

2 tablespoons harissa (see page 44)

2 large tomatoes

4 merguez lamb sausages

3 tablespoons purple kalamata olives

½ bunch flat-leaf parsley

- Peel the potatoes and cut them in large chunks. Finely chop the garlic and cut the onion into half-moon slices. Heat a generous splash of olive oil in a large frying pan. Sauté the garlic, onion, and harissa for about 5 minutes on low heat. Add the potatoes. Quarter the tomatoes and add them to the pan. Let the stew simmer for about 15 minutes, then add some water to help make a sauce, and season with salt.
- Grill the sausages for about 5 minutes in a cast-iron grill pan or in the oven.
- Add the sausages and olives to the stew. Finely chop the parsley and stir into the stew just before serving.

You don't always need meat to make a tasty köfte. Using potato, bulgur, walnuts, and Turkish paprika paste, you can create the same seasoned, rich flavor sensation as when making a köfte with ground beef. The dish is topped off with some fresh sour sumac yogurt. So easy!

Potato Köfte

With Turkish paprika paste, walnuts, and sumac yogurt

SERVES 4

1¼ pounds (500g) Yukon gold potatoes

Scant 1 cup (150 g) fine bulgur (see page 22)

¾ cup (75g) walnuts, chopped

5 tablespoons (75 g) Turkish paprika paste (see page 44)

Mild olive oil

1 tablespoon sumac (see page 148)

1¾ cups (400 g) thick Turkish or Greek yogurt (see page 126)

- Preheat the oven to 400°F (205°C). Place the unpeeled potatoes in a large pot and cover with generously salted water. Bring to a boil and cook until they're tender, about 30 minutes for medium-size potatoes.
- Allow the potatoes to cool slightly, then peel them. In a large bowl, mash the potatoes together with the bulgur, walnuts, paprika paste, and a pinch of salt.
- With your hands, form the mix into köftes (small cylinder shapes about 4 inches/10 cm long and 1¼ inches/3 cm thick in the center) and place them on a baking sheet. Brush with some oil and bake for 15 to 20 minutes, until crisp and heated through.
- In a small bowl, stir together the sumac and yogurt and season with salt. Serve the sumac yogurt alongside the köftes.

Sesame is one of the oldest cultivated plants on earth. Throughout history, magical powers have been attributed to this plant. Open sesame! Rightly so, for how could we live without sesame, and therefore without tahini? We are addicted! The main ingredient of tahini is ground sesame seed, and it should be only the best-quality sesame seed, namely the one from Ethiopia (although there are other varieties).

You will find many different brands of tahini, both imported and domestic, in supermarkets, health-food stores, and Middle Eastern groceries. In Lebanon, Egypt, and most other Middle Eastern countries, they make tahini from lightly toasted sesame seeds. It is sold in plastic jars. The Turkish variety differs in that it's made with dark toasted seeds. It's sold in glass jars. Brands made here in the States are available roasted or not, salted or unsalted, and are sold in both glass jars and cans. You will have to try them to find your favorite.

How to eat tahini

In addition to being served in, over, and alongside hummus, tahini is also wonderful mixed with a little pekmez (grape syrup), carob syrup, honey, or pomegranate molasses and served as a dip for fresh bread, dried figs, or fruit. All of these syrups are readily available in Middle Eastern groceries.

We also like to make a smooth, delicious salad dressing by mixing tahini with some boiling water, lemon juice, and salt. Don't make the mistake of mixing tahini with cold water, because you'll get punished right away: It'll turn to glue. Tahini is delightful with grilled meat, grilled fish, and grilled vegetables, especially grilled or deep-fried cauliflower! Honestly, tahini tastes great with almost everything. Simply dip some dried figs in tahini—irresistible!

Halva: sesame nougat

Sesame halva (or helwa) is made from sesame paste, sugar syrup, and egg white (sometimes common soapwort is also used as an emulsifier). It's a type of sesame nougat with a rather loose structure, a bit like fudge. Sometimes pistachios are mixed in (our favorite), or cacao. You can find halva in Middle Eastern groceries. To eat it, you have to break it into chunks. It tastes great with a cup of strong tea, which can be addictive in itself. (Yes, we do say that a lot.)

White tahini—made from hulled sesame seeds that are lightly toasted—is unsurpassed, but hard to come by. It comes in two different qualities: the "royal" tahini, which is made from the highest-quality stone-ground sesame seeds, and the "regular," which is machine-ground.

"It sells like helwa." These things fly over the counter!

TAHINI

The Middle Eastern white tahini is the defining flavor in hummus—no tahini, no hummus. Dating back to the thirteenth century, tahini is a truly traditional Middle Eastern ingredient.

Eggplant and tahini make one of those culinary marriages that withstand the test of time. This combination of eggplant, fruity green herbs, lemon zest, crunchy almonds, and creamy cheese is irresistible. Wonderful for an Arabia buffet or as a lunch dish. Beyaz peynir is traditional fresh, white sheep's-milk cheese from Turkey. It is easy to make at home, or look for it (sold in cans) in Middle Eastern groceries and online. You can substitute feta cheese, although it's saltier.

Grilled Eggplant

With fresh herbs, almonds, and tahini dressing

SERVES 4 TO 8

4 firm, long eggplants

Mild olive oil

4 sprigs oregano

4 sprigs basil

5 sprigs flat-leaf parsley

½ cup (50 g) blanched almonds

¾ cup (180 ml) white tahini (see page 58)

Grated zest and juice of 1 lemon

½ cup (75 g) white Turkish cheese (beyaz peynir, see page 126) or feta cheese

Fruity green olive oil

Aleppo pepper (see page 44)

- Preheat the oven to 400°F (205°C). Thinly slice the eggplants lengthwise. Sprinkle the slices with salt and drizzle with mild olive oil. Place them on a baking sheet and roast for about 15 minutes, until golden brown.
- Pick the herbs. Heat a small amount of mild olive oil in a skillet and gently toast the almonds until golden brown. Allow to cool and chop them coarsely. Make a dressing with the tahini, lemon juice, 6½ tablespoons (92 ml) boiling water, and some oil. Season with salt. The hot water will ensure that the dressing stays liquid. If the dressing thickens, add some more hot water and season with some extra salt.
- Lay the roasted eggplant slices on a platter and allow them to cool down a bit. Lavishly sprinkle with the herbs, lemon zest, and almonds. Crumble the cheese over the eggplants and drizzle them with the tahini dressing and some fruity green oil. Season with a pinch of Aleppo pepper.

We won't elaborate on this recipe: After all, how hard can it be to buy some ready-made halva from the Middle Eastern grocery and mix it with some tahini? Stick it in the freezer. Wait one night. Done. Your patience will be rewarded with divine pleasure. Serve this in small portions because it's very rich (and very delicious).

Tahini-Halva Ice Cream

SERVES 8 TO 10

1 pound (500 g) halva (see page 58)

⅔ cup (165 ml) white tahini (see page 58)

- Pick the halva you like best, with or without pistachios, and break it into small chunks. In a mixing bowl, stir the halva, first using a fork and then a wooden spoon, adding small amounts of tahini at a time, until the mixture is smooth.
- Spoon into a sealable plastic container and leave it in the freezer—don't stir—for at least one night, allowing it to turn into smooth ice cream.

افتح يا سمسم (جنجلان)

Sesame is one of the oldest cultivated plants on earth. Throughout history, magical powers have been attributed to this plant.
Open sesame!

Here is another recipe in which tahini plays the lead role. The combination of grilled cauliflower and tahini is something you won't easily forget. We added some preserved lemon for that extra kick. This salad has everything to make one happy: crunchy bread, earthy lentils, nutty tahini, and zesty preserved lemon peel. Mix everything together just before serving to keep the bread crunchy.

Salad of Roasted Cauliflower

With lentils and tahini dressing

SERVES 4

1 small head cauliflower

Mild olive oil

¼ pan bread (see page 251) or another rustic bread (about 4 ounces/110 g)

½ cup (100 g) Le Puy (French green) lentils (see page 82)

2 bunches flat-leaf parsley

½ preserved lemon (see page 34)

¾ cup (180 ml) white tahini (see page 58)

1 clove garlic

Juice of 2 lemons

Fruity green olive oil

- Preheat the oven to broil. Cut the cauliflower into florets and then thinly slice the florets. Place them in an ovenproof dish and toss with some mild olive oil and salt. Shred the bread into small pieces and drizzle with oil before adding to the cauliflower. Roast the cauliflower and the bread for about 10 minutes, until golden brown.

- In the meantime, cook the lentils for about 20 minutes, until al dente. Pick the leaves and the young stems from the parsley; roughly chop and set aside. Quarter the preserved lemon, remove the pulp, and thinly slice the peel; set aside. Mix together the tahini, lemon juice, 6½ tablespoons (92 ml) boiling water, and some mild olive oil to make a dressing. Push the garlic through a press into the dressing and season with salt. The hot water will ensure that the dressing stays liquid. If the dressing thickens, add more water and season with extra salt.

- At the very last moment, combine the cauliflower and croutons with the lentils, parsley, and preserved lemon. Generously sprinkle with tahini dressing.

Tahini is the ultimate Arabian ready-made ingredient: It tastes great with everything and makes everything taste great. This breakfast dish is fantastic and it takes hardly any effort, except for shopping to find a delicious Middle Eastern white tahini, a tasty pekmez (a molasses-like syrup made from condensed grapes or figs), and freshly baked simit. Dip and done. Heavenly.

Tahini and Pekmez

With crunchy simit

SERVES 2 TO 4

¾ cup (180 ml) white tahini (see page 58)

6½ tablespoons (92 ml) pekmez

Fresh simit (see page 250) or another type of freshly baked crusty, seeded bread

• Stir the tahini in a little bowl and pour in the pekmez. Dip your bread and eat. This is perfect with a cappuccino, a latte, or an Arabian coffee.

Nutty spices

Sesame, poppy seed, nigella seed (black seeds used mostly for bread), mahleb (the pits of tart cherries, used in desserts and pastry, sold at Middle Eastern grocery stores).

Storage

Keep your spices tightly sealed. If you want to keep them longer, you can put them in the freezer in plastic bags. If your spices have lost their freshness, you can revive their spirit by toasting them in a dry skillet until they become fragrant.

Fresh and hot spices

All sorts of peppers, sumac, pink pepper, paprika, tamarind, Aleppo, laos, fenugreek, malagueta pepper, and pimento. Also mastic (meska horra, the aromatic resin from the mastic tree), which we use to lend structure and to season dishes. It's like a natural chewing gum. Ask for it at your local Middle Eastern grocery store.

Warm spices

Cinnamon (both ground and in sticks), cumin seed, coriander, saffron, anise seed, fennel seed, ginger, clove, juniper berries, rose petals, vanilla, star anise, cardamom, caraway, nutmeg, mace, turmeric, pimentón.

Centuries old

For centuries spices have been used as medicine, preservative, and magic potion to embellish dishes with flavor. They play a critical role in the Arabian cuisine. A kitchen filled with a wide variety of spices is something to show off. Look at what I have! Expensive saffron from Iran, a wonderful selection of peppers, and many, many different intoxicating spices from the far corners of the world!

Your own baharat

As a rule of thumb, you can say that warm spices always mix well together. Adding a spice or two from the "fresh and hot" category is nice, too. This way you can mix your own baharat melanges (or spice mixes) a little differently every time. Or sprinkle some crunchy, lightly toasted cumin seed, fennel seed, or anise seed over a dish. This is always lovely as a crunchy flavor enhancer or a finishing touch. You should get a small spice or coffee grinder and a motar and pestle; nothing is more delightful than the smell of your own freshly ground spice mixtures.

Crude oil

In the old days spices were what crude oil is today: an important and valuable commodity for which the Western world was dependent on the Eastern world. Not to mention the dubious role some Westerners (our Dutch ancestors prominently among them) played in this lucrative trade.

SPICES

Measuring

We measure spices in tablespoons instead of teaspoons! Taste while you're cooking and season to your own preferences.

This is *the* way to make the most out of leftover spices. Use these spice-and-salt mixtures to season nuts, eggs, grilled fish, tajines—whatever you like. We discover new possibilities every day. Be generous with spices and less so with salt: Spices are flavor enhancing!

Seasoned Salt

CORIANDER-ANISE SALT

2 tablespoons coriander seed

1 tablespoon anise seed

Coarse sea salt

CUMIN SALT

3 tablespoons ground cumin

Coarse sea salt

CARAWAY-CUMIN-CHILE SALT

1 tablespoon caraway seed

2 tablespoons cumin seed

1 tablespoon Aleppo pepper or red pepper flakes (see page 44)

Coarse sea salt

FENNEL SALT

2 tablespoons fennel seed

Coarse sea salt

- CORIANDER-ANISE SALT

  Using a mortar and pestle, coarsely grind the coriander and the anise seed with some salt.

- CUMIN SALT

  Using a mortar and pestle, coarsely grind the cumin with some salt.

- CARAWAY-CUMIN-CHILE SALT

  Using a mortar and pestle, coarsely grind the caraway, cumin, and pepper with some salt.

- FENNEL SALT

  Using a mortar and pestle, coarsely grind the fennel with some salt.

Kamal Mouzawak first prepared this dish for us and we've eaten it many times since at Tawlet in Beirut, a restaurant that is part of Souk el Tayeb, the farmer's market Kamal created. It is the quintessential spice-celebrating dessert. Its flavor is intense and you either love it or you hate it. In the Middle East this restorative dessert is often served as special nourishment for women who've just given birth. It's certainly worth a try. After all, anise seed is well known in the Netherlands as part of another tradition of welcoming newborn babies: *beschuit met muisjes* (breakfast biscuits with sprinkles). Note that the nuts are to be soaked overnight.

Meghli

With spices

SERVES 8 TO 10

½ cup (60 g) blanched almonds

½ cup (60 g) shelled pistachio nuts

1½ teaspoons caraway seed

1 teaspoon anise seed

¾ cup (150 g) sugar

2 teaspoons cinnamon

⅔ cup (100 g) rice flour

Grated zest of 1 lemon

Grated zest of ½ orange

- Place the almonds and pistachios in separate bowls and cover with cold water. Let the nuts soak overnight. The next day, drain and coarsely chop them.
- Bring 4½ cups (1 L) water to a boil. Finely grind the caraway and the anise seed with a mortar and pestle. Combine them in a mixing bowl with the sugar, cinnamon, and rice flour, then stir in 1 cup (240 ml) cold water. Add the citrus zest. Whisk the resulting slurry into the boiling water, bring to a boil once more, and then lower the heat and cook for about 30 minutes over low heat, stirring frequently with a wooden spoon to keep the mixture from sticking to the bottom of the pan, until the mixture is thick, the consistency of warm pudding.
- Divide the meghli into small bowls and allow to cool (the pudding will solidify, but remain wobbly). Cover the meghli with plastic wrap and store it in the fridge. Before serving, sprinkle with the soaked almonds and pistachios.

The quince season is fleeting, from October till December, so we buy these lovely fruits as soon as we see them. They are bulky, pear-like fruits that smell wonderful sitting in the fruit bowl. They're great for making jam, to stew in tajines, or to make into these spicy-sweet quince wedges. Sometimes the skin can be quite furry—scrub them thoroughly before using. These are delicious with ice cream or yogurt, or in a lamb tajine with pumpkin.

Cinnamon—Star Anise Quinces

SERVES 4 TO 8

1½ cups (300 g) sugar

2 cinnamon sticks

5 star anise

Zest of ½ lemon

4 quinces

- Add 2 cups (480 ml) water to a large pan. Add the sugar, cinnamon, anise, and lemon zest, and bring the mixture to a boil.
- Quarter the unpeeled quinces and remove the cores. Add the quinces to the syrup in the pan and top them with a plate to ensure they remain submerged. Over low heat, boil them for about 30 minutes.
- Either allow the quinces to cool off in the syrup, or serve them warm. You decide.

Sellou and *sfouf* are very much alike; in fact, the names used for this unbaked Moroccan sweet are often interchangeable—the more compact sellou is basically sfouf with a little extra oil. Both are a mixture of spices, sugar, and roasted flour. With some nuts, we turn it into a tantalizing "dessert-cookie" (a term we coined) or a little snack from Moroccan cuisine. Sellou is traditionally eaten during Ramadan, when celebrating newborn babies, and on other festive occasions. It's wonderful with saffron tea. Take care when buying saffron: It should always be expensive. If not, you have mediocre saffron on your hands. It should be of a deep red color and the aroma should be intoxicating, even when smelled through the wrapper. The high price of this spice makes sense: It takes between 200,000 and 400,000 hand-picked saffron crocuses to harvest 2½ pounds (1 kg) of saffron. Fortunately, if you buy good quality, you need very little.

Saffron Tea

With sellou

SERVES 6 TO 10

For the sellou:

4 cups (500 g) all-purpose flour

2 tablespoons cinnamon

2 tablespoons fennel seed

2 tablespoons anise seed

1 cup (100 g) chopped hazelnuts

1⅓ cups (315 ml) walnut or almond oil

Confectioners' sugar

- Preheat the oven to 400°F (205°C). Spread the flour out on a rimmed baking sheet in a thin, even layer and roast for 35 to 40 minutes, until light brown. While roasting, frequently stir with a long wooden spoon, allowing the flour to toast evenly. One minute before taking the flour out of the oven, add the cinnamon, fennel seed, and anise seed.

- Add the spice-flour mix and the hazelnuts to a food processor and pulse until finely ground. Slowly pour in the oil and blend until fully incorporated. Add confectioners' sugar and salt to taste. Form the mixture into a nicely flattened mound on a platter or plate. Hand out little bowls and let everyone serve themselves. Eat with small spoons.

- SAFFRON TEA
  Put a small pinch of saffron in a teapot and pour about 4½ cups (1 L) boiling water over it. Let it steep for a while. If you wish, you can season the tea with a little honey. You can also use green tea instead of boiling water for a less pronounced saffron flavor. Serve the saffron tea in small glasses or cups.

We can trace the use of spices for their healing properties to ancient China and the philosophy of ying and yang. This knowledge was brought to the Middle East and North Africa in the earliest days of the spice trade. These fries are good for you! Cumin contains plenty of magnesium and iron (good for the digestion) and fennel seed bursts with vitamins A, B, C, and E. When you use cumin you can cut back on salt because cumin fortifies the taste of salt. These fries are inspired by Moroccan cumin fries. We boil the potatoes beforehand and then fry them in the oven with oil, so they're crispy on the outside and tender on the inside. Want to bet that you'll keep on eating? (By the way, according to Arabic and European tales from the Middle Ages, cumin helps you have a stable love life. People used to carry cumin with them during weddings.)

Cumin Fennel Fries

SERVES 4 TO 8

3 pounds (1½ kg) large Yukon gold potatoes

Mild olive oil

2 tablespoons fennel seed

2 tablespoons cumin seed

- Scrub the potatoes but don't peel them. Cut the potatoes into thick fries and boil in a large pot of generously salted water for about 10 minutes, until nearly tender. Let drain.
- Preheat the oven to 425°F (220°C). Arrange the fries on a baking sheet and drizzle generously with olive oil. Bake for about 15 minutes, until golden brown.
- Crush the fennel and cumin seed in a mortar and pestle with some coarse salt and sprinkle over the fries.

Food for the poor

Lentils are another great example of food for the poor.
They don't need to be soaked. Arabic lentils are regular brown
lentils or Le Puy–like (French green) firm lentils. A well-known
dish from the Middle East is mujaddara, which is bulgur or rice
mixed with lentils and lots of crispy, brown fried onions on top.
It is simple and incredibly delicious. Lentils are wonderful in salads,
they are a great combination with tahini, and they are yummy with
rice and bulgur. They are essential in kushari, a combination of
lentils, rice, and pasta that began as peasant food in Egypt.
Lentils are readily available and they keep for a long time.

Chickpeas come in two types:
desi and kabuli; the latter are lighter
in color and have a smoother coat.
We've noticed that there can be a big
difference in quality of chickpeas:
the fresher the chickpeas (meaning
they've been dried for a shorter time
after the harvest), the better. A nice
cooked chickpea is nutty, creamy,
firm, and not mealy—a real treat.
Buy dried chickpeas in a market
where the stock turns over quickly;
that's where chances for "fresh"
dried chickpeas are highest.

Cooking chickpeas

Besides our mission for self-steamed couscous,
we also crusade for home-cooked chickpeas. No
more canned beans: They are too mealy, overcooked,
and acidic, which means They're not suitable for salads, let alone for warm dishes or hummus. Cooking
chickpeas is easy: Soak them overnight in ample
water, and then boil them in clean water for about
45 minutes (depending on how long you've soaked
them and whether they are old or young), and let
them cool. If you wish to always have them on hand,
you can freeze them after soaking or after cooking.

Super smooth hummus

You get the best hummus by cooking the soaked chickpeas with 1 teaspoon baking powder or a piece of kombu (edible kelp or sea vegetable; discard it after use). This softens the skin and improves the taste; it also makes them easier to digest.

CHICKPEAS & LENTILS

Desi and kabuli

Chickpeas may be the oldest ingredients: They were cultivated more than ten thousand years ago in what's now Syria and Turkey. You can keep chickpeas for a long time; they are incredibly nutritious and can be used in many ways.

Iraqi cuisine is still mostly unknown territory for us. We are familiar with masgouf, smoked fish from the banks of the Tigris, and the delicious kebab made with extra fatty lamb, but that's about it. What we *do* know is that Baghdad was the center of (culinary) civilization during the Middle Ages. This recipe stems from those days and tantalizes with spices and rose water, which was a common ingredient in the savory dishes of European royal kitchens.

Iraqi Madfuna

SERVES 4

¾ cup (135 g) dried chickpeas (soaked overnight, see page 82)

2 (about 1 pound/450 g total) eggplants

3 onions

Mild olive oil

2 tablespoons coriander, divided

2 tablespoons cinnamon, divided

2 pinches saffron

1¼ pounds (500 g) ground lamb

Rose water (see page 92)

- Boil the chickpeas in ample water for about 45 minutes, until tender. Halve the eggplants, scoop out the pulp (see Note), and set them aside.
- Halve the onions and slice them. Heat a good amount of olive oil in a large, deep skillet, add the onions, 1 tablespoon of the coriander, 1 tablespoon of the cinnamon, and all of the saffron. Let cook for about 15 minutes, then add the chickpeas and remove from the heat.
- Combine the lamb with the remaining coriander and cinnamon, and season with salt. Fill the eggplant halves with the lamb mixture. Place them on top of the chickpea-onion mixture and add water until they float. Season with salt.
- Partially cover the pot and bring to a simmer. Stew the eggplants for about 30 minutes. Carefully remove them from the pan and cover to keep warm. Continue to cook the onion broth for about 5 minutes to reduce slightly. Add a few drops of rose water to taste. Serve the eggplants with the chickpea-onion mixture.

NOTE: Reserve the pulp of the eggplants. It's delicious when sautéed in olive oil with garlic and served with tahini, olive oil, and parsley.

We learned to make this rustic peasant dish in Lebanon, where, to our surprise, they not only eat it for dinner, but also for breakfast! Our most recent favorite place was a tiny hole in the wall in the Gemmayze section of Beirut, where you can eat divine fetteh in enormous quantities. It doesn't look very impressive at first, but wait until you've had your very first fetteh experience, then we'll talk!

Fetteh

With chickpeas

SERVES 4

1¼ cups (300 g) chickpeas (soaked overnight, see page 82)

2 flatbreads (Arabic flatbreads, or 4 pita breads, see page 250)

4 tablespoons (55 g) butter, divided

Mild olive oil

2 cups (500 g) thick, 3 percent fat Turkish or Greek yogurt (see page 126)

1 clove garlic, minced

½ cup (65 g) pine nuts

Sprigs of mint, for serving

1 large sweet onion, cut into wedges, for serving

Pickled turnips (see page 112), for serving

- Boil the chickpeas in ample water for about 45 minutes. Tear the flatbreads in large pieces. Heat 1 tablespoon of the butter with a dash of olive oil in a skillet and sauté the bread pieces until crispy and golden brown. Remove from the heat, sprinkle with some salt, and set aside.

- In a saucepan, warm the yogurt over low heat, stirring constantly; do not let it boil. Stir in the garlic and season with salt.

- In a small frying pan, heat the remaining butter and sauté the nuts until golden brown.

- Divide the flatbread pieces among four bowls, spoon the chickpeas on top, and scoop the garlic-yogurt mixture over them. Garnish with the pine nuts and butter. Serve with sprigs of mint, onion wedges, and pickled turnips.

What's left to say about hummus? We're addicted to it. For you, it might be the reason to begin loving Arabia cuisine. Be aware: There's hummus, and there's hummus. Once you've tasted silk-soft, velvet-creamy hummus, you can't go back to prepared hummus (and yes, that includes hummus made from canned chickpeas). Soak those chickpeas, turn on that food processor, and use quality tahini. We promise you'll be rewarded with much love from the hummus police. In this recipe, we sprinkle some dukkah, an Egyptian mixture of spices and nuts, on top. It's not traditional, but it does taste lovely.

Lebanese Hummus

With Egyptian dukkah

SERVES 4 TO 8

2½ cups (500 g) chickpeas (soaked overnight, see page 82)

1 teaspoon baking powder

⅔ cup (165 ml) white tahini (see page 58)

1 clove garlic

Lemon juice

Fruity green olive oil

Arabia's Dukkah (page 164)

- Rinse the chickpeas. Put them in a large pan and add water until they are about ¾ inch (2 cm) submerged. Add the baking powder and bring to a boil. Cover and cook the chickpeas for 2 to 3 hours, until very tender. Let cool and then drain, reserving some of the cooking liquid.
- Pulse the chickpeas with the tahini, garlic, salt, and some lemon juice in a food processor. Pulse until the mixture has a velvety texture (be patient—this can take 15 to 20 minutes). Add some water during the process, to make the hummus smooth. Season with more lemon juice and salt.
- Spoon the hummus on a plate, use a spoon to trace a few nice grooves, and drizzle generously with olive oil. Sprinkle dukkah on top.

The cuisine of Gaza is very rich, with distinctive flavors such as this combination of dill seed with red hot chile peppers. It makes this lentil stew delicious. Serve with crusty rustic bread or pita bread.

Fukharit'adas

Lentil stew from Gaza with dill pepper oil

SERVES 4 TO 6

3 small dried red chile peppers

4 tablespoons (36g) dill seed

2 cloves garlic

2 tablespoons cumin seed

¾ cup (180 ml) fruity green olive oil

2 Yukon gold potatoes

2 cups (400 g) brown lentils (see page 82)

- Coarsely chop the peppers, then crush them with a mortar and pestle along with the dill seed, garlic, cumin seed, and some coarse salt. Stir in the olive oil.
- Peel the potatoes and cut them in large chunks. In a large pot of water, boil the lentils with the potatoes until tender about 30 minutes. Drain. Stir in the dill-pepper oil and season with another splash of olive oil and some coarse salt.

Flavor-enhancing orange blossom water

In the Middle East and the Maghreb, orange blossom (or orange flower) water is mostly used in cookies and desserts. In the Maghreb they also use orange blossom in hearty meals like tajine or couscous dishes. Look for it in small bottles in the baking aisle of Middle Eastern grocery stores (with other extracts), or order it online. It is delicious in puddings, like muhallabia and zriga, and cookies, but it's also surprisingly good in tajine with lamb and chicken, as well as our new favorite, water with lemon juice and cucumber. In Lebanon, we were delighted with white coffee: hot water with orange blossom water. It does wonders for the digestion. In Libya, we were offered an espresso with a dash of orange blossom water. Use orange blossom water sparingly at first, because you'll need to get used to the strong taste and scent.

The taste of roses

Rose water has also been used in the kitchen since the Middle Ages. Rose water is distilled from the pink Damascus rose, which is very aromatic and has an abundance of petals. Rose water is used to flavor Turkish delight (Turkish lokum). It has a strong taste and fragrance and it's best used in small amounts (the uninitiated will quickly associate it with soap). Its uses are as varied and plentiful as the petals of a Damascus rose. It used to be common to use rose water in savory meals (in highly spiced meat dishes in Iraq, for example; see the recipe on page 84), but nowadays in Arabia cuisine you see rose water mostly in sweets. Rose water can also be found in Middle Eastern grocery stores, in baking specialty shops, and online.

Perfume

Orange blossom water was already being used in Spain in the fourteenth century to perfume linens. In the seventeenth century it was used in abundance in European cuisines. The blossom of the bitter orange—from which orange blossom water is distilled—is a symbol of fertility.

ORANGE BLOSSOM & ROSE WATER

This is a great culinary marriage: Watermelon and rose water are simply made for each other. When frozen, the subtle flavors of each come out and the rose water gives the watermelon a kick. You can also pour a dash of ice-cold vodka over the granita. This is delicious in between the mezze and the main course, and also as a dessert or a "pick-me-up" on a warm summer day.

Watermelon Granita

With rose water

SERVES 6 TO 8

1¼ pounds (500 g) watermelon

Rose water (see page 92)

Sugar, optional

- Slice the rind off the watermelon and remove all seeds. Cut into pieces and place in a blender with rose water to taste. Process into a smooth puree (you can also use a hand blender). Taste and add some sugar if it needs sweetening; if you really don't taste the rose water, add some more. The flavor can be quite pronounced at this point because it will diminish during freezing.
- Put the mixture in a plastic container and let freeze for 4 to 6 hours. With a fork, scrape and stir the granita every hour to get small, pretty ice crystals.

This is another classic Moroccan condiment. It's one that we can easily make from the food in our pantry because we usually have all the ingredients on hand. It is delicious with grilled meat, grilled fish, and grilled chicken, and also spread on a piece of grilled rustic bread.

Tomato Chutney

With honey, sesame seeds, and orange blossom water

SERVES 4 TO 6

2 onions

Mild olive oil

2½ pounds (1 kg) ripe cherry tomatoes

Grated zest of 1 lemon

¾ cup (180 ml) honey

1 cup (150 g) raw white sesame seeds

Generous splash of orange blossom water (see page 92)

- Cut the onions into half-moon slices. In a large frying pan, heat some olive oil and sauté the onions for about 10 minutes over low heat. Quarter the tomatoes and add them along with the lemon zest. Sauté for another 20 minutes.
- Add the honey, season with some salt and, at the last moment, stir in the sesame seeds and the orange blossom water.

Orange blossom water is the delightful ingredient in white coffee (hot water with orange blossom water) and also in these drinks. The cucumber water is divinely refreshing on warm days or during an elaborate dinner (orange blossom water is excellent for digestion), and the date sauce is a real kick-starter when you want more energy. We like to have it for breakfast.

Cucumber Water and Date Sauce
With orange blossom water

SERVES 6 TO 8

CUCUMBER–ORANGE BLOSSOM WATER

½ cucumber

Orange blossom water (see page 92)

DATE SAUCE WITH ORANGE BLOSSOM WATER

Handful of pitted medjool dates

4½ cups (1 L) freshly squeezed orange juice

Orange blossom water (see page 92)

½ teaspoon cinnamon

• CUCUMBER–ORANGE BLOSSOM WATER

Peel the cucumber in small strokes and bind the peels together with cooking twine or a cucumber ribbon; discard (or eat) the peeled cucumber. Put the peels in a jar, add a small splash of orange blossom water, and top off the jar with ice-cold water. If you wish you can add some ice cubes. Taste and add more orange blossom water, if desired.

• DATE SAUCE WITH ORANGE BLOSSOM WATER

Quarter the dates. Soak them for about 30 minutes in the orange juice with a small dash of orange blossom water added. Add the cinnamon and mix in a blender until smooth. Serve very cold. For a lighter version you can strain the juice and discard the solids.

THE ENTIRE STREET SMELLS OF ORANGE BLOSSOM

In Morocco, the smell of orange blossom lingers throughout the entire spring season. It will waft right into your car when you have the windows open. At every souk there are women selling fresh blossoms, and it seems that everyone is busy distilling their essence. Suddenly, the cobbler's store changes into a distillery with beautiful copper kettles to separate the orange blossom oil (neroli) and orange blossom water (the water that remains behind). In Morocco and Turkey we would often get bunches of fresh orange blossom on our pillows as a sign of hospitality. The fresh blossom is also delicious in tea.

Nothing pairs better with the heady fragrance of seductive rose water than a meringue. These meringues are crispy on the outside and chewy on the inside. The tart-sweet pomegranate arils are an excellent companion—just like the beautiful napkins—made for us by our dear friend, designer Marije Vogelzang.

Rose Meringue

With pomegranate arils

SERVES 6 TO 8

Lemon juice or vinegar

6 egg whites

1½ cups (300 g) granulated sugar

1 tablespoon cornstarch

Rose water (see page 92)

1 pomegranate

Confectioners' sugar, if desired

- Preheat the oven to 250°F (120°C). Make sure the bowl and whisk of a stand mixer (or handheld electric mixer) are oil free by cleaning them with some lemon juice or vinegar on a paper towel. Add the egg whites to the bowl and, on medium speed, beat them until just thickened. Add one-third of the granulated sugar and beat on a higher speed. Add another one-third of the sugar and beat until the sugar has dissolved. Add the remaining sugar and beat on the highest speed until the foam is shiny and forms stiff peaks. Take care not to overbeat or the meringue will collapse. With a wooden spoon, stir in the cornstarch and between 1 tea-spoon to 1 tablespoon (depending on your taste) of rose water. The more rose water, the stronger the flavor, and you'll risk seeing rose water leak from the meringues.
- Line a baking sheet with parchment paper and arrange dollops of meringue any way you wish. You can even form fanciful peaks of foam, but don't make them too big. Bake the meringue for about 2 hours.
- Peel the pomegranate. Cut off the crown and break the pomegranate open with your thumbs. Remove the arils, making sure the white pith doesn't come along. Let the meringues cool, then sprinkle with pomegranate arils and some confectioners' sugar for a nice coating, if desired.

This is a super simple delight. White cabbage and grated carrot are perfect ingredients for a salad. Combined with tarragon and orange blossom vinaigrette, this salad magically turns into a mouthwatering pleasure.

White Cabbage–Carrot Salad

With tarragon and orange blossom water

SERVES 4 TO 6

½ head white (or light green) cabbage

1 large carrot

2 bunches tarragon (or 1 bunch each parsely and mint)

2 oranges

Mild olive oil

⅓ cup (75 g) pine nuts

Orange blossom water (see page 92)

Fruity green olive oil

• Coarsely grate the cabbage and carrot. Tear the herb leaves from the sprigs and cut them coarsely. Peel the oranges and remove as much of the white pith as possible. Holding an orange over a bowl to collect the juice, slice the orange segments away from the membrane and cut each segment in half. Repeat with the second orange. Set the segment and the juice aside.

• In a skillet, heat a good amount of mild olive oil and roast the pine nuts until golden brown. Set aside to cool. In a large bowl, mix the cabbage, carrot, tarragon, the orange segments and juice, and a splash of orange blossom water. Add fruity green olive oil and coarse salt to taste. Before serving, mix in the pine nuts.

Pickling

Pickled vegetables are very important in Arabic cuisine. Even the pickled capers from Sicily and Sardinia had already appeared in Arabic cookbooks during the tenth century, although they originally came from the Greeks. In medieval times, the Arabs reintroduced them to Europe. People still pickle many vegetables in the Middle East today, and not only to keep the abundance of the summer harvest for winter. It's a delicious treat to have plenty of tangy, salty, crispy peppers, cucumbers, carrots, cabbage, or bits of turnips to nibble with all kinds of Arabic dishes from breakfast to dinner. We love to pickle our own vegetables and it's not complicated. It's best to use a mix of sour and salt (sea salt, never table salt!), so the vegetables remain crunchy and don't become too sour. We boil the jars or put them in a hot dishwasher and allow them to dry well. Once filled, we place the jars in direct sunlight first to get the fermentation process going and then we put them away in a cool, dark place.

The Ottomans

You can trace the culinary influence of the power-thirsty Ottomans by following their dolma and sarma from country to country to see how far their empire spread. First, some clarification: A dolma is not a stuffed grape leave, but a stuffed anything, although usually a vegetable, like a scooped-out and stuffed zucchini, eggplant, bell pepper, or tomato. A stuffed, rolled-up grape, cabbage, or beet leaf is a sarma. There are endless variations on stuffings, but the most well-known sarma or dolma stuffing is cooked rice with meat. Eat them warm or cold. We find the Lebanese grape-leaf sarmas the prettiest and tastiest. They are made with a lot of care and attention. They're beautiful, thin, tightly rolled "cigars" of young grape leaves.

Gossip

Do you know the best thing about stuffing sarmas? The more you do it, the better you get. Stuffing sarmas is the time for gossip in Arabic kitchens. The latest marriages, divorces, and other family gossip are discussed and commented on at length. Before you know it, hundreds of sarmas have been stuffed.

Pickling capers

When we're on vacation in a Mediterranean country, we search among the rocks and shrubs for nice, low caper bushes, with their distinctive round leaves, pretty buds, and purple flowers (though when you see flowers, you know you're too late!). Surrounded by thorns, we picked the flower buds, the capers. At home we rinse them and put them in a jar with ample coarse sea salt. They are delicious after only a few days! We make use of the caper salt as well; it has a nice flowery taste.

Your own grape leaves

If you have a profusely growing grape vine in your garden (or your neighbor's), you can pickle your own grape leaves. Every season at Georgina Al Bayeh's restaurant Tawlet, we saw the kitchen table filled with heaps of fresh picked grape leaves. Blanch them quickly in salted water, dab them dry, make a nice stack, put them in zip-top plastic bags, and freeze them. You can also pickle them (put them in a jar with heavily salted water) and keep them in the fridge.

GRAPE LEAVES,
PICKLED VEGETABLES
& CAPERS

Pickling vegetables (*mouneh*) is a tradition from the mountains of Lebanon. It's easy to make your own mixed pickles: They're delicious with all kinds of dishes and a staple of the mezze. It's also essential with fetteh and other peasant dishes.

Cucumbers and Sweet Peppers

Stuffed and pickled

MAKES ABOUT A
1-QUARTER (960-ML)
JAR OF EACH

PICKLED CUCUMBERS

2 cups (480 ml) white wine or apple cider vinegar (see Note)

1 pound (500 g) small, firm cucumbers

3 hot green peppers

2 tablespoons dill seed

STUFFED PICKLED SWEET PEPPERS

2 cups (480 ml) white wine or apple cider vinegar (see Note)

3 cauliflower florets

½ cup (50 g) walnuts

2 small carrots

8 red sweet Italian peppers

PICKLED CUCUMBERS

- Bring 2 cups (480 ml) water to a boil with 3 tablespoons coarse sea salt. When the salt has dissolved, let it cool a little, then mix with the vinegar. Scrub the cucumbers thoroughly but do not peel. Clean the hot peppers by slicing them open and removing the seeds.
- Fill scalded glass jars (see page 112) with the cucumbers and the peppers until the jars are almost full. Sprinkle the dill seed on top. Pour the hot salt-and-vinegar water in the jar. If the vegetables aren't submerged, prepare more salt-and-vinegar water in the same proportions. Put the lid on and place the jar in front of a window or outside for about 4 days, so they'll get some sunlight.
- Move the jar to the fridge. Keep refrigerated.

PICKLED SWEET PEPPERS

- Make the salt-and-vinegar water brine as above. Finely chop the cauliflower florets, walnuts, and carrots. Cut the tops off the sweet peppers, scrape out the seeds, and stuff them with cauliflower, walnuts, and carrots. Fill the scalded glass jars (see page 112) in the same manner with the stuffed sweet peppers and the salt-vinegar water and preserve as above.

NOTE: If you prefer crisper pickles, use more vinegar than water.

These grape-leaf rolls are a funky variation on the traditional sarma. Instead of cooked rice, bulgur, or tabouleh, we use labneh (strained yogurt) with nuts, mint, and tarragon as a filling. Round up some people to help you roll and gossip (that's the tradition when you make *warak enab*, as these are called in Arabic). Eat them immediately, while the nuts are still crispy. These are delicious as part of your mezze.

Grape-Leaf Rolls

With labneh, nuts, tarragon, and sumac

MAKES 18 TO 20 ROLLS

18 to 20 medium-size grape leaves (in a jar, see page 106)

4 tablespoons (60g) pine nuts

4 tablespoons (25g) shelled pistachio nuts

2 sprigs mint

3 sprigs tarragon

½ tablespoon sumac (see page 148)

¼ cup (50 g) fine bulgur (see page 22)

½ cup (120 g) thick Turkish or Greek yogurt (see page 126)

- Blanch the grape leaves in boiling water for 2 minutes and let drain on a clean kitchen towel. Roast the pine nuts and pistachio nuts in a dry frying pan. Let cool and chop fine.
- Pick the mint leaves and tarragon and chop very fine. In a mixing bowl, combine the pine nuts, pistachio nuts, mint, tarragon, sumac, bulgur, and yogurt, and season with salt.
- On a clean work surface, spread out a grape leaf in front of you and cut out the stem. Place a little bit of stuffing (about 1 tablespoon) near the edge and form into a cylinder. Fold in the sides of the leaf and roll from the bottom as nicely and tightly as you can. Repeat until you've used all the stuffing. Cover and refrigerate for 30 minutes before serving to let the bulgur soften.

A few important rules to prevent mold in your pickled vegetables:

- Use clean canning jars that you can close tightly. If they have metal lids, place some plastic wrap on top of the jar before you screw on the lid. That way the salt-vinegar water won't touch the metal.

- Sterilize the jars. Clean them in the dishwasher on the highest temperature, or boil them for a few minutes in a large pot of water. Let the jars dry upside down.

- Always use clean utensils to fill the jars or to take vegetables out; otherwise you'll still get mold.

- If you have a lot of jars, label them by date so you know which ones to eat first.

You can keep most pickled vegetables for at least six months in the refrigerator.

Pickled Turnips

SERVES 8 TO 10

2 cups (480 ml) white or apple cider vinegar

10 small turnips

1 small beet

2 sprigs oregano

- Bring 2 cups (480 ml) of water to a boil with 3 tablespoons coarse sea salt. Let cool for a bit and mix with the vinegar. Peel the turnips and beet and cut in wedges.
- Fill a sterilized jar with the turnips, beet, and oregano until the jar is almost full. Pour the salt-vinegar water in the jar. If the jar isn't filled to the top, make more salt-vinegar water in the same proportion.
- Let sit in the refrigerator for at least 2 weeks before opening.

Across the Middle East, lamb is always eaten highly seasoned. The meat itself has a pretty strong flavor, and it won't be easily dominated by all the flavor enhancements you add to it. You'll find capers everywhere in the Arabic world and across the Mediterranean, but Italians are the largest consumers. This dish is also wonderful prepared on a hot outdoor grill with the lid on.

Lamb Chops

With salted capers and an oregano bread-crumb crust

SERVES 4

3 tablespoons salted capers

3 sprigs thyme

3 sprigs oregano

⅛ pan bread (see page 251) or another rustic bread (about 2 ounces/55 g)

½ clove garlic, chopped

About 2 tablespoons mild olive oil

Freshly ground black pepper

8 lamb chops (not too thin)

• Preheat the oven to 400°F (205°C). Wipe most of the salt from the capers (but don't throw it away; it's delicious on a boiled egg or to finish off your pasta). Pick the thyme and oregano leaves.

• In a food processor, grind the bread with the capers, thyme, oregano, and garlic until you have fine crumbs. Mix in a generous splash of olive oil and season with some freshly ground black pepper.

• Place the lamb chops on a lightly oiled baking sheet and arrange the crumbs over them. Roast the lamb chops for 10 to 12 minutes, until the meat is medium-rare and the crumbs are crisp.

NOTE: If you can't find salt-cured capers, you can use capers in brine, well drained. Be sure to taste the bread-crumb mixture: It should be very flavorful and quite salty; add more salt if needed.

Thank you for not soaking!

We're going to be strict from now on: Stop soaking couscous. In our eyes, it's sacrilege. When you only soak your couscous in hot water or bouillon, you'll end up eating sticky couscous that isn't light and fluffy at all. However, when you prepare couscous the traditional way—steaming the granules three times—they will change into light, golden yellow, tasty, gooey little pearls that fall apart like loose grains of sand. It makes a Sahara of difference. Wouldn't you be willing to make an effort for that? First buy a large *couscoussière,* a steam pan consisting of a large pan for the broth with a steam basket for the couscous placed on top. Couscoussières are sold at kitchen supply stores and larger Middle Eastern grocery stores. Just go for a large one. That way you can steam a pound or two of couscous at once, which takes the same effort as doing smaller portions anyway. Also buy a large flat round platter or dish, which can be used for loosening the couscous granules by hand. It's a wonderful feeling, kneading the warm granules with your hands. Now that's complete relaxation! Any leftover cooked couscous can simply be stored in the freezer. Then you need to steam it only once to warm it up when you need it later. You can read how to steam couscous on the following pages.

A well-formed grain

Couscous, seksu, and *ta'am*—all have the same meaning: "well formed"; and they refer to the dish itself. Couscous is made from coarse semolina (coarsely ground wheat flour), fine semolina, and water. In the past, the granules were hand rolled by women—what a chore! Today you can buy instant couscous in any store, but beware: There is a big difference in quality. Your best option is a quality brand from a Middle Eastern grocery store. Couscous is eaten in all the Maghreb countries, but also on the Italian islands of Sicily and Sardinia. Sardinian *fregula* pasta, Lebanese *moghrabieh,* and Palestinian *maftoul* are all derived from couscous and *mhamsa* (a coarse couscous with larger granules, often called Israeli couscous).

Many varieties

Fine couscous is used for sweet dishes, for dishes with delicate sauces, and for stews. Medium couscous is used in traditional vegetable and meat dishes. Coarse (whole-wheat) couscous is used in peasant dishes, just like belboula, which is made from pearl barley. This couscous originates from the Sahara, where it's predominantly eaten in combination with camel meat and milk. Corn couscous is made from a mixture of one-half corn flour and one-half medium-fine wheat flour. This golden yellow couscous is a little more gooey and sweet.

With buttermilk and butter

Season the warm couscous by kneading in sumptuous amounts of butter, smen, or olive oil with your hands. During the summer, people in the Middle East love to have *saykouk* (buttermilk couscous), served in glasses. It may sound odd, but the combination is delightful! Buttermilk is often also consumed in combination with savory dishes, such as couscous with chicken. Sometimes the milk is served separately; sometimes it's mixed in with the couscous in little bowls.

COUSCOUS

Not so long ago we discovered couscous made from corn: a golden-colored, gooey couscous with a rich flavor. We steam this couscous only twice; more really isn't necessary. We love to combine couscous with vegetables and other flavor-enhancing ingredients, something that the Moroccans probably wouldn't do, but something you can definitely surprise them with.

Corn Couscous

With preserved lemon, saffron, and artichoke

SERVES 4

1 cup (200 g) chickpeas (soaked overnight, see page 82)

2¼ cups (350 g) corn couscous (see page 116)

Mild olive oil

3 tablespoons butter, divided

4 fresh artichokes

2 large sweet onions

2 pinches saffron threads

½ preserved lemon (see page 34)

- Boil the chickpeas for 45 minutes, or until al dente.
- Meanwhile, bring plenty of water to a boil in the bottom pan of a couscoussière. (If you don't have one, use a skewer or thin nail to poke a few dozen holes in the bottom of a round aluminum foil cake pan. Put water in the bottom of a large saucepan and push the cake pan down into the saucepan so that the lip of the cake pan is held by the rim of the saucepan and keeps it suspended over the water like a steamer. If necessary, mold the foil pan to make it fit. Wrap the pot lid in a towel if it doesn't fit snugly over the foil pan to prevent too much steam from escaping.) Sprinkle the couscous with 6½ tablespoons (92 ml) warm water, ½ teaspoon salt, and 1 tablespoon olive oil and use your hands to loosen the granules, gently rolling them between your fingers. Place the couscous in the top compartment of the pan and steam it for about 10 minutes. Ladle the couscous into a large bowl, let it cool, and sprinkle again with 3 tablespoons water. As soon as the heat is bearable, separate the granules, gradually rolling any lumps between the palms of both hands in a circular motion. Steam the couscous once more for 10 minutes, then spoon it into a large bowl. Stir to loosen, then fold in the butter and chickpeas and cover to keep warm.
- Rinse the artichokes and clean them, trimming part of the stem and peeling the rest. Trim about three-quarters of the flower leaves and peel the artichoke all around like an apple. Scoop out the purple leaves and the choke from the inside with a spoon and neatly trim the base. Keep the artichokes submerged in water with some lemon juice. Cut the onions into half-moon slices. Heat a good amount of olive oil with a pinch of the saffron, add the onions, and sauté over medium heat until well browned, about 15 minutes. Slice the artichoke hearts and add them to the onions with 2 cups (480 ml) water, a pinch of salt, and the rest of the saffron. Cook for 20 more minutes.
- Scrape the pulp from the inside of the preserved lemon and thinly slice the peel. With a slotted spoon, lift the artichoke mix out of the pan and into the couscous mixture, reserving the broth. Fold in the strips of preserved lemon peel and season with a pinch of salt, if needed. Serve the saffron broth separately.

This isn't a traditional Maghreb-style fish couscous, which is usually accompanied by a tomato sauce in which the fish was cooked. Instead, we cooked our fish in a hearty fennel bouillon. The tomatoes were transformed into aromatic caramelized cherry tomatoes with anise, cinnamon, and orange blossom water.

Couscous with Hake

And fennel bouillon and preserved orange blossom tomatoes

SERVES 4

9 ounces (250 g) cherry tomatoes

1 tablespoon cinnamon

1 tablespoon anise seed

Orange blossom water (see page 92)

3 onions

1 clove garlic

1 lemon

Mild olive oil

2 fennel bulbs

2¼ cups (350 g) medium couscous (see page 116)

1¼ pounds (600 g) hake or Pacific cod fillets, with skin

- Preheat the oven to 200°F (90°C). Halve the tomatoes and place them, face up, on a baking sheet; sprinkle them with the cinnamon, anise seed, and some salt and let them dry in the oven for about 4 hours. For the last hour, generously drizzle with orange blossom water.
- Coarsely chop the onions and the garlic. Remove the peel (without the pith) from the lemon. Heat a good amount of oil in a Dutch oven, and cook the onions, garlic, and lemon peel for about 10 minutes over low heat. Chop the fennel, reserving the green fronds for later. Add the fennel to the pot and generously season with salt and pepper; add enough water to cover the fennel. Cover the pot and let everything simmer for 30 minutes.
- Bring ample water to a boil in the bottom pan of the couscoussière. Sprinkle the couscous with 6½ tablespoons (92 ml) warm water, some salt, and 1 tablespoon olive oil. Use your hands to loosen the granules, gently rolling them between your fingers. Place the couscous in the top compartment of the pan and steam it for 10 minutes. Ladle the couscous into a large bowl, let it cool, and sprinkle again with 3 tablespoons of water. As soon as the heat is bearable, separate the granules gradually, rolling any lumps between the palms of both hands in a circular motion. Steam the couscous again for 10 minutes. Roll the granules to separate again. Add salt and oil to taste. Steam the couscous a third time.
- Meanwhile, sprinkle the fish with salt and pepper. Heat a layer of oil in a skillet and fry the fish, skin side down, until the skin is crisp but the fish is not yet tender. Take the fish out of the skillet and put it into the fennel broth for about 5 minutes to cook through. Remove the lemon peel, add half of the fennel fronds, and season with salt, pepper, and lemon juice.
- Mix the steamed couscous with a little of the fennel broth. Ladle into a large dish and arrange the fennel stew, the fish, and the dried tomatoes on top of the couscous. Sprinkle the rest with a little chopped fennel frond. Drizzle with some orange blossom water and olive oil. Serve the rest of the broth separately.

This really is a couscous in the Italian Sardinian style, using typical Sardinian flavors like saffron and fennel seed. All the ingredients are mixed together according to the Sardinian tradition, resulting in a delicious, light couscous. It's a bonus if you can find the light-green, firm, small zucchini, but the regular ones are nice as well.

Zucchini Couscous

With pistachios, saffron, and lemon zest

SERVES 4

2¼ cups (350 g) medium couscous (see page 116)

Mild olive oil

3 small light-green zucchini (or one regular zucchini)

2 sweet onions

1 clove garlic

Grated zest of 1 lemon

2 tablespoons fennel seed

2 pinches saffron threads

½ tablespoon crushed red pepper flakes or Aleppo pepper (see page 44)

1 cup (100 g) shelled pistachio nuts

- Bring ample water to a boil in the bottom pan of a couscoussière. Sprinkle the couscous with 6½ tablespoons (92 ml) warm water, some salt, and 1 tablespoon olive oil. Use your hands to loosen the granules, gently rolling them between your fingers. Place the couscous in the top compartment of the pan and steam it for 10 minutes. Ladle the couscous into a large bowl, let it cool, and sprinkle again with 3 tablespoons water. As soon as the heat is bearable, separate the granules gradually, rolling any lumps between the palms of both hands in a circular motion. Steam the couscous again for 10 minutes. Loosen again and add salt and oil to taste. Steam the couscous one last time. Before serving, use a wooden spoon to thoroughly stir and separate the couscous.
- Slice the zucchini and cut the onions into half-moon slices. Mince the garlic. Heat a good amount of olive oil in a large skillet and sauté the onions, garlic, lemon zest, fennel seed, and saffron for 10 minutes over low heat. Add the zucchini and ¾ cup (180 ml) water. Let simmer for another 20 minutes, then add the crushed red pepper.
- Toast the pistachios for 2 minutes in a hot, dry skillet. Let cool and chop coarsely. Ladle the zucchini-onion mixture from the broth and fold it in with the couscous. Fold in the pistachios. Drizzle some broth over the couscous and serve the rest in a separate bowl.

This nutritious couscous with spicy meatballs and sweet butternut squash was a wonderful surprise for us! Recently we discovered Indian coriander seed: very large seeds of a light-green color with a citrus-coriander flavor. See if you can find them yourself; they're worth the effort!

Belboula Couscous

With butternut squash, harissa, coriander, and spicy ground-lamb meatballs

SERVES 4

2¼ cups (350 g) belboula (barley) couscous (see page 116)

Mild olive oil

1 butternut squash

2 cloves garlic

4 tablespoons (36 g) harissa (see page 44), divided

1 tablespoon (36 g) Aleppo pepper (see page 44), divided

4 tablespoons coriander seed, divided

14 ounces (400 g) ground lamb

1 bunch cilantro

- Bring ample water to a boil in the bottom pan of a couscoussière. Sprinkle the couscous with 6½ tablespoons (92 ml) warm water, some salt, and 1 tablespoon olive oil. Use your hands to loosen the granules, gently rolling them between your fingers. Place the couscous in the top compartment of the pan and steam it for 10 minutes. Ladle the couscous into a large bowl, let it cool, and sprinkle again with 3 tablespoons of water. As soon as the heat is bearable, separate the granules gradually, rolling any lumps between the palms of both hands in a circular motion. Steam the couscous again for 10 minutes. Separate the grains again and add salt and oil to taste. Steam the couscous one last time. Before serving, use a wooden spoon to meticulously separate the couscous.
- Peel the butternut squash, remove the seeds, and cut into large chunks. Mince the garlic. Heat up a good amount of oil and sauté the squash with the garlic, 2 tablespoons of the harissa, ½ tablespoon of the Aleppo pepper, and 2 tablespoons of the coriander seed; cook, stirring constantly, until very fragrant, 2 to 3 minutes. Add 2½ cups (600 ml) water and simmer for 10 minutes over low heat. Meanwhile, knead the ground lamb with the remaining harissa, Aleppo pepper, coriander seed, and some salt. Roll into 1-inch (2.5-cm) meatballs and add these to the squash stew. Cover the pot and cook for another 10 minutes.
- Finely chop the cilantro and stir it into the stew. Serve the belboula couscous with the squash and the lamb meatballs on top.

زيت الزيتون
olive oil

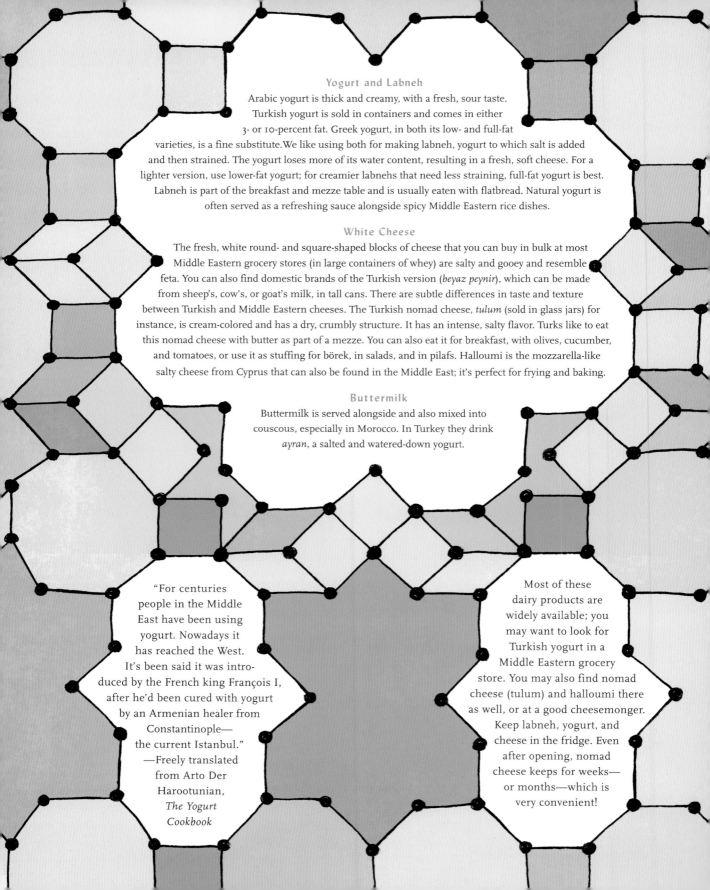

Yogurt and Labneh

Arabic yogurt is thick and creamy, with a fresh, sour taste. Turkish yogurt is sold in containers and comes in either 3- or 10-percent fat. Greek yogurt, in both its low- and full-fat varieties, is a fine substitute. We like using both for making labneh, yogurt to which salt is added and then strained. The yogurt loses more of its water content, resulting in a fresh, soft cheese. For a lighter version, use lower-fat yogurt; for creamier labnehs that need less straining, full-fat yogurt is best. Labneh is part of the breakfast and mezze table and is usually eaten with flatbread. Natural yogurt is often served as a refreshing sauce alongside spicy Middle Eastern rice dishes.

White Cheese

The fresh, white round- and square-shaped blocks of cheese that you can buy in bulk at most Middle Eastern grocery stores (in large containers of whey) are salty and gooey and resemble feta. You can also find domestic brands of the Turkish version (*beyaz peynir*), which can be made from sheep's, cow's, or goat's milk, in tall cans. There are subtle differences in taste and texture between Turkish and Middle Eastern cheeses. The Turkish nomad cheese, *tulum* (sold in glass jars) for instance, is cream-colored and has a dry, crumbly structure. It has an intense, salty flavor. Turks like to eat this nomad cheese with butter as part of a mezze. You can also eat it for breakfast, with olives, cucumber, and tomatoes, or use it as stuffing for börek, in salads, and in pilafs. Halloumi is the mozzarella-like salty cheese from Cyprus that can also be found in the Middle East; it's perfect for frying and baking.

Buttermilk

Buttermilk is served alongside and also mixed into couscous, especially in Morocco. In Turkey they drink *ayran*, a salted and watered-down yogurt.

"For centuries people in the Middle East have been using yogurt. Nowadays it has reached the West. It's been said it was introduced by the French king François I, after he'd been cured with yogurt by an Armenian healer from Constantinople— the current Istanbul." —Freely translated from Arto Der Harootunian, *The Yogurt Cookbook*

Most of these dairy products are widely available; you may want to look for Turkish yogurt in a Middle Eastern grocery store. You may also find nomad cheese (tulum) and halloumi there as well, or at a good cheesemonger. Keep labneh, yogurt, and cheese in the fridge. Even after opening, nomad cheese keeps for weeks— or months—which is very convenient!

YOGURT, DAIRY
& CHEESE

In the Arab world yogurt is savory.
Yogurt, or laban, is eaten with
dinner and comes in several
varieties. Cheese is usually fresh
and salty white cheese, except the
Turkish nomad cheese, which is
dried and aged, and the hard-to-
find Lebanese kishk, which is
dried and fermented labneh.

Yogurt is lovely as a dressing, which you might already know from tasting the cold yogurt combination served over grilled eggplant in the dish moutabbal, a staple in the Arab world. We replaced the eggplant with zucchini and fennel, and paired them with peppery watercress, crunchy almonds, and citrus fruit, all of which taste wonderful with the yogurt. We processed some of the watercress with the yogurt, which adds extra punch to the dressing. This would be delicious with a spicy fish dish like Samak Harra (page 50).

Grilled Vegetables

With watercress yogurt and crunchy almond oil

SERVES 4 TO 6

1 zucchini

1 fennel bulb

2 oranges

2 lemons

1 cup (250 g) yogurt (see page 126)

5¼ ounces (150 g) watercress

Mild olive oil

¾ cup (75 g) almonds

- With a mandoline, thinly slice the zucchini and the fennel bulb; reserve the fennel fronds. Heat a grill pan and grill the zucchini and fennel slices until light brown on both sides.
- Peel the lemons and the oranges, making sure to remove as much of the pith as possible. Cut the lemon and orange wedges loose from their membranes.
- Using a hand blender, process the yogurt, half of the watercress, and a pinch of salt.
- Add ample mild olive oil to a small deep skillet and fry the almonds until light golden brown. Let them cool, sprinkle with salt, then process with the hand blender until you get a crunchy, oily mixture. Arrange the fennel and the zucchini slices on a dish, then spoon the lemon and orange wedges and the rest of the watercress on top. Generously drizzle with the watercress-yogurt dressing and the crunchy almond oil.

In Lebanon and the Middle East they really like to eat labneh (savory strained yogurt) as part of a mezze table. Over the years we've become true "labnehstas," so we've come up with several delicious flavors of our own. Our friends in Lebanon think it's weird, but they wolf down our concoctions nonetheless. With lovely fresh flatbread it's a great mezze, and it's also delicious for lunch!

Arabia's Labneh

SERVES 4

BASIC LABNEH
1 cup (250 g) Turkish or Greek yogurt (low- or full-fat)

LABNEH WITH ANISE SEED, TOMATO SEEDS, AND GREEN PEPPER
Labneh
2 tablespoons anise seed
1 very ripe tomato
1 green bell pepper
Fruity green olive oil

LABNEH WITH ANISE SEED, ROSE PETALS, AND POME-GRANATE ARILS
Labneh
2 tablespoons anise seed
2 tablespoons dried edible rose petals
½ pomegranate
Fruity green olive oil

LABNEH WITH ZA'ATAR, PARSLEY, AND SESAME SEEDS
Labneh
3 tablespoons Za'atar (page 168)
2 tablespoons finely chopped flat-leaf parsley
2 tablespoons raw white sesame seeds
Fruity green olive oil

LABNEH WITH CRUNCHY HAZELNUTS AND CITRUS ZEST
Labneh
4 tablespoons roasted hazelnuts
Grated zest of ½ lemon
Grated zest of ½ orange
Fruity green olive oil

- BASIC LABNEH

Stir some coarse sea salt into the yogurt. Line a colander with a clean kitchen towel or cheesecloth and place it in a large bowl. Spoon in the yogurt and allow to strain for 4 hours. Spread the strained yogurt on a nice platter or plate. With a spoon, smooth the surface and make a few circular grooves on top.

- LABNEH WITH ANISE SEED, TOMA-TO SEEDS, AND GREEN PEPPER

Sprinkle the labneh with the anise seed. Squeeze out the tomato, sprinkling the seeds and juice over the labneh (you can use the rest of the tomato for something else). Trim the top off the green bell pepper and roll it between the palms of your hands to remove and discard the seeds and the pith. Mince the pepper and sprinkle it on top of the labneh with a little coarse sea salt, then generously drizzle with oil.

- LABNEH WITH ANISE SEED, ROSE PETALS, AND POMEGRANATE ARILS

Sprinkle the labneh with anise seed. Crumble the dried rose petals. Seed the pomegranate, making sure not to scoop out the white membranes. Sprinkle the labneh with the rose petals and pome-granate arils and generously drizzle with oil.

- LABNEH WITH ZA'ATAR, PARSLEY, AND SESAME SEED

Sprinkle the labneh with the za'atar, parsley, sesame seed, and a pinch of coarse sea salt. Generously drizzle with oil.

- LABNEH WITH CRUNCHY HAZELNUTS AND CITRUS ZEST

Finely chop the nuts and mix with the citrus zest. Sprinkle over the labneh with a pinch a coarse sea salt and gener-ously drizzle with oil.

At the Souk el Tayeb in Beirut, we always see the most wonderful balls of pickled labneh. They're not hard to make at home—a little patience and attention are all that's needed! These look great on a mezze table and are delicious, too.

Pickled Labneh

SERVES 4 TO 6

5 cups (1 kg) Turkish or Greek yogurt (low-fat)

Mild olive oil

Grated zest of 1 lemon and/or 1 orange

Sumac (see page 148)

Dried mint

Dried oregano

Shelled pistachio nuts

Aleppo pepper (see page 44)

- Line a colander with clean cheesecloth (or a clean, thin kitchen towel) and place it over a large bowl. Stir 2 tablespoons salt into the yogurt, then spoon the yogurt into the colander. Gather up the edges the cheesecloth to form a bundle. You can use some string to tie it together if you like. Place in the fridge and let it strain for 3 days, occasionally throwing out the excess whey from the bowl. Transfer the yogurt to a large platter and let it dry slightly, outside of the fridge, for a few hours. With lightly oiled hands, roll the labneh into little (about ¾-inch/2-cm) balls. Place on an oiled platter and let the labneh balls firm up in the fridge for a few hours.

- Meanwhile, prepare one or more flavorings of your choice. Mix the lemon and/or orange zest with some sumac to taste and roll several labneh balls through the mixture until completely coated. Mix some mint with an equal amount of oregano. Roll a couple of the labneh balls through the mixture until completely coated. Finely chop the pistachios and mix with some Aleppo pepper. Roll the remaining labneh balls through the mixture until completely coated.

- Put all the different labneh balls in a large, sterilized glass canning jar (see page 112) and fill the jar to the top with olive oil. Cover and store in a cool, dark place or in the fridge. Leave for a few weeks, allowing the flavors to develop nicely. Are you impatient? No worries. They're also great when you eat them right away! Serve with some bread.

Loubnan, Arabic for Lebanon, is derived from *laban*, which means yogurt. It represents the country's permanently snowcapped mountains, and the Lebanese love to eat it, too.

These eggs are originally Turkish, but you will find savory, warm yogurt served throughout the entire Middle East. It's a delightful lunch and brunch dish, and also makes for an easy dinner.

Fried Eggs
With warm garlic yogurt

SERVES 4

Mild olive oil

4 fresh large eggs

1 clove garlic

1 cup (250 g) full-fat Turkish or Greek yogurt

3 sprigs mint

Grated zest of 1 lemon

Fruity green olive oil

- Heat a splash of mild olive oil in a skillet and fry the eggs over low heat (until the yolk is either runny or well done, as you prefer).
- Finely grate the garlic over the yogurt, add some salt to taste, and mix thoroughly. Divide the yogurt over the eggs in the skillet and warm briefly.
- Mince the mint leaves. Slide the eggs and the warm yogurt onto a large plate, or divide among four small plates. Sprinkle with mint, lemon zest, and some extra salt, if needed. Generously drizzle with fruity green oil. Delicious with Turkish pide bread, flatbread, or pita.

A thousand and one seeds

The pomegranate is not only very beautiful, it's also very delicious. The arils, as the seeds are called, are good in all kinds of salads, in yogurt, in meat dishes—in everything! We love the job of cutting out the crown with a small sharp knife, breaking the pomegranate, peeling out the arils one by one, and removing the bitter white pith. The pomegranate arils vary in color from light to dark pink and from tart to sweet (the lighter ones are sweeter and softer), but they are always fragrant. With care, you can keep a pomegranate for a few weeks. The skin and arils will dry out a little but it will still taste good.

Pomegranate molasses

Pomegranate molasses—the thick, condensed juice from the sweet and tart pomegranate—is almost comparable to a good, aged balsamic vinegar. It is a syrupy, dark, sweet-tart, complex molasses that is essential for the Middle Eastern bread salad fattoush, but also delicious over chicken with meat, and in all kinds of sauces and dressings. Pomegranate molasses with sumac is a classic combination. Pomegranate molasses is sold in glass bottles in Middle Eastern groceries, by upscale food retailers, and online. The Turkish variety is much sweeter and more syrupy; it is less complex taste-wise, and has a translucent light-brown color. The Middle Eastern variety is deep, dark red, or even black, and has a tart, complex taste. Once you've tasted the real molasses, you'll want nothing else. The best is homemade pomegranate molasses that you buy locally in the countries of origin. We have a tart molasses made by nuns in a cloister in Syria (in a Pepsi-Cola bottle), and from a family in the Lebanon mountains we got a gasoline can full of their own pomegranate molasses, in which we taste the flavor of roses. Sold!

The pomegranate is treasured by all cultures

To the ancient Greeks, Persephone with her pomegranate was the first herald of spring and the hope for a good harvest (later interpreted as a symbol of abundance). For Jews, pomegranate arils are a symbol of the 613 commandments of the Torah. Christians see the pomegranate as a symbol of the resurrection of Christ, and the Koran mentions the pomegranate three times as a symbol of all the good that Allah has created; it grows in the gardens of Paradise. In ancient Persia, the pomegranate was a symbol of fertility, and the Bedouins of the Middle East also use it as such at weddings. The pomegranate tree could in fact be the original tree of life described in the Bible.

Grenadine

The pomegranate is a major component of Middle Eastern cuisine, from the sweet-tart pomegranate molasses in Lebanon, Syria, and southern Turkey, to sweet-tart juice and arils in stews like fesenjan (chicken stew) in Iran and Iraq. In northern Africa, Italy, and Spain, the pomegranate is mostly consumed as a fruit and juice. Grenadine syrup is also derived from the pomegranate.

POMEGRANATES & POMEGRANATE MOLASSES

The ultimate seduction: a sweet aphrodisiac par excellence. The combination of pomegranate molasses, rose water, orange blossom water, and almond paste is sublime. These are nice with coffee or tea, and also as dessert.

Stuffed Dates

With almond-pomegranate paste and orange blossom and rose water

MAKES 25 PIECES

¾ cup (75 g) blanched almonds

⅓ cup (75 g) sugar

2 tablespoons fruity green olive oil

2 tablespoons pomegranate molasses (see page 138)

Orange blossom water (see page 92)

Rose water (see page 92)

25 dates

Pomegranate arils

- Using a food processor, grind the almonds with the sugar, olive oil, pomegranate molasses, and a few drops each of orange blossom and rose water; process into a soft, smooth paste. Sample the paste. Should it taste a bit more tart? Then add some pomegranate molasses. Should it be more fragrant? Add some orange blossom and rose water.

- Divide the paste into 25 small balls. Slice the dates open from one side (don't cut them all the way through) and stuff them with the paste. If you wish, you can sprinkle them with some pomegranate arils.

Here too pomegranate molasses plays the lead role, sprinkling its fairy dust over its red-colored friends, the beets. Earthy, sweet, tart, and complex, the cardamom-orange zest gives this dish a special kick. The aromatic orange zest is also lovely with a bit of leftover white cheese or labneh for breakfast.

Roasted Beets

With pomegranate molasses, white cheese, and candied cardamom-orange zest

SERVES 6 TO 8

10 young beets

Fruity green olive oil

1 large orange

1¼ cups (250 g) sugar

5 cardamom pods, or 1 tea-spoon ground cardamom

2 cups (300 g) Turkish white cheese (beyaz peynir, canned, see page 126) or feta cheese

Pomegranate molasses (see page 138)

• Preheat the oven to 400°F (205°C). Trim the tops of the beets, peel, and cut them in wedges. Arrange on a baking tray, sprinkle with some salt, and drizzle with olive oil. Roast the beets for 40 minutes.

• Meanwhile, use a zester to peel thin strips of orange zest, or slice off the skin with a small sharp knife and julienne. In a small pot, boil the orange zest in ample water for 3 minutes. Drain, cover with fresh water, and boil once more for a few minutes. Drain again.

• In another small pot, add the sugar to ⅔ cup (165 ml) water and bring to a boil. If using cardamom pods, remove the black seeds from the pods and finely grind the seeds with a mortar and pestle. Add the cardamom and the orange to the sugar syrup. Let it boil down over low heat until the zest is saturated. Remove the zest from the syrup and let dry on a plate. Save the syrup for another use.

• Before serving, crumble the cheese over the warm or cold beets and gar-nish with the candied zest. Drizzle generously with olive oil and pome-granate molasses.

Sweet yogurt is an exciting combination for those in the Middle East who are used to savory flavors. The fusion of these intense ingredients makes for a passion-filled dessert.

Anise Yogurt

With pomegranate molasses, pomegranate, and passion fruit

SERVES 4

2 cups (500 g) Turkish or Greek yogurt (see page 126)

2 tablespoons anise seed

Pomegranate molasses (see page 138)

4 passion fruits

8 tablespoons (85 g) pomegranate arils

• Divide the yogurt among four bowls. Sprinkle with the anise seed and drizzle generously with the pomegranate molasses. Scoop the flesh of the passion fruits on top and sprinkle with the pomegranate arils.

This is a must: a delicious blend of doughy olive-oil focaccia, tart berries, spinach, and sweet, pungent Roquefort cheese, finished off with sweet-tart pomegranate molasses. Pair this with a full-bodied red wine for an irresistible combination. Look for dried barberries (Iranian berries or *zereshk*) in Middle Eastern grocery stores or order them online. If you don't have dried barberries or cranberries, sprinkle a little sumac (see page 148) over the focaccia before adding the spinach.

Focaccia

With spinach, Roquefort cheese, and pomegranate molasses

SERVES 6 TO 8

1 tablespoon fresh yeast, or 1 teaspoon instant yeast

4 cups (500 g) all-purpose flour

6 tablespoons (90 ml) mild olive oil, plus more for the pan and drizzling

2 small onions

8 ounces (225 g) fresh spinach

⅓ cup (50 g) barberries, or dried cranberries

5 ounces (150 g) Roquefort cheese

Pomegranate molasses (see page 138)

- Dissolve the yeast in 1 cup (240 ml) lukewarm water. Put the flour in the bowl of a food processor or stand mixer fitted with the paddle attachment, add 1 tablespoon salt, the oil, and the yeast water and process for about 10 minutes on medium speed, until the mixture becomes a batter-like dough. Grease a medium bowl with some oil and pour the dough in. Cover with a clean, moist kitchen towel and let rise in a warm, draft-free spot for about 1½ hours, until the dough has risen slightly.
- Lightly grease a large round or square baking pan—at least 10 inches (25 cm) across—with olive oil and spread the dough out in an even layer of about ¾ inch (2 cm); let it rest for 30 minutes.
- Preheat the oven to 400°F (205°C). Drizzle the dough with some olive oil and bake for 25 to 30 minutes, until golden brown.
- Slice the onions. Heat a good amount of olive oil in a cast-iron skillet and sauté the onions until tender and golden, about 10 minutes. Add the spinach and sauté, turning with tongs, until it is evenly wilted, about 3 minutes. Add the berries and sauté until they're a little swollen, about 3 minutes. Season with some salt and pepper. Arrange the spinach and the Roquefort over the warm focaccia, and drizzle to taste with some pomegranate molasses. The cheese will melt a little.
- Slice the focaccia in wedges and serve immediately, or let it cool—it's still delicious one day later!

Beautiful red spice

Sumac is a spice derived from the dried ground berries of a bush that grows throughout the Mediterranean and the Middle East. Ground sumac varies in color from purple-red to burgundy-red; it varies in quality as well. Sumac has a tangy and aromatic flavor, and you can use it as you would ground pepper—simply pepper a dish with it. Traditionally, it is sprinkled over fried eggs, grilled chicken, and salads like fattoush, and it's often used in combination with pomegranate molasses for thick, sweet-tart dressings. You can buy sumac in Middle Eastern grocery stores, gourmet shops, and from online spice merchants. Always purchase the best quality!

No lemons? Use sumac!

Ground sumac has a sweet, tangy taste. In summer, when there are no lemons in the Middle East, they use it instead of lemon juice. Simply stir water into the sumac to make a juice.

SUMAC

This is a serendipitous recipe. It's fantastic as a festive appetizer and also does well as part of a buffet. Stuffed grape leaves are usually rolled, but these baked grape-leaf bundles are nice and simple—no need for parchment paper or aluminum foil. They're a bit crispy, which makes them extra delicious.

Grape-Leaf Bundles

With cherry tomatoes and sumac

SERVES 4

10½ ounces (300 g) cherry tomatoes on the vine

5 ounces (150 g) Turkish white cheese (beyaz peynir, canned, see page 126) or feta cheese

½ cup (75 g) wrinkled black olives

16 large grape leaves (rinsed from a can or homemade, see page 106)

1 tablespoon dried mint

1 tablespoon sumac (see page 148)

Mild olive oil

- Preheat the oven to 400°F (205°C). Cut the tomatoes into 8 portions. Crumble the cheese into small chunks. Pit the olives. Dab the grape leaves dry.

- On a large, lightly greased baking sheet, place 2 grape leaves next to and on top of each other so they form 1 larger leaf. Repeat with the remaining leaves. Arrange the tomatoes, cheese, and olives over the leaves, sprinkle with mint and sumac, and fold up into bundles. Sprinkle the bundles with some salt flakes, if you wish.

- Lightly drizzle the bundles with some olive oil and bake for 5 to 8 minutes in the center of the oven, until the edges of the leaves become crispy.

Chicken with spicy, tangy sumac is a classic dish in Lebanon, Jordan, and Syria, and the combination of pomegranate molasses and coarse black pepper is our personal favorite addition. Toum (a traditional Middle Eastern garlic sauce) is an integral part of the dish; garlic is ground with salt and lemon juice to form a light emulsion (similar to mayonnaise). We roast the garlic first to soften it. A whole chicken cut open along its back and flattened is also perfect for this recipe, especially when you roast it on the grill.

Sumac Chicken

With lemon, pomegranate molasses, and toum

SERVES 4

3 lemons

2 tablespoons black peppercorns

8 chicken drumsticks or thighs

3 tablespoons sumac (see page 148), divided

Mild olive oil

1 garlic bulb

Pomegranate molasses (see page 138)

- Preheat the oven to 500°F (260°C) . Cut 1 lemon in thin slices and squeeze the others for their juice. Crack the peppercorns with a mortar and pestle. Mix the chicken legs with a big splash of lemon juice, 2 tablespoons of the sumac, the peppercorns, a generous splash of olive oil, and about 2 teaspoons salt flakes. Place the chicken on a baking sheet and bake in the center of the oven for about 15 minutes, until the skin is golden brown.

- Slice the top off the garlic bulb and place it in the middle of some aluminum foil. Pour some olive oil over the top and fold the aluminum foil around the bulb. Lower the temperature of the oven to 350°F (175°C). Arrange the slices of lemon over the chicken. Add the wrapped garlic bulb to the baking sheet with the chicken, and return it to the oven for about 45 minutes, until the chicken is cooked through and very tender.

- Remove the garlic from the foil, let it cool, and pop the soft garlic gloves from their skin. Sprinkle the chicken legs with the remaining sumac, drizzle with pomegranate molasses, and let it rest in the oven (it should be turned off, but it will still be warm).

- With a hand blender or with the mortar and pestle, puree the roasted garlic with a dash of lemon juice, a dash of cold water, and some salt to taste; blend into a thick, smooth sauce. Serve the chicken with pomegranate molasses and the toum. Serve with pickled vegetables and peppers (see page 106) and fresh flatbread or pita bread.

The best *kibbeh nayeh* is the one we eat in Ehden, Lebanon, while enjoying a fantastic view from the mountains. The one and only real kibbeh nayeh is made from raw goat meat mixed with some fine bulgur, but raw lamb or veal, fresh and of the best quality, works too. You could compare it to steak tartare, which also is raw ground meat seasoned with spices and flavor enhancers. You eat it with olive oil, sea salt, and crisp cucumber, radishes, and scallions. It's also delicious as part of the mezze. We have added rose petals and ginger for an exotically flavored kibbeh nayeh. Ask your butcher to grind the meat three times.

Kibbeh Nayeh

With rose petals and sumac

SERVES 6 TO 8

14 ounces (400 g) very fresh raw ground veal or ground lamb

2 tablespoons dried edible rose petals (available at baking supply shops and online)

2 tablespoons sumac (see page 148), divided

1 tablespoon ground ginger

½ cup (100 g) fine bulgur (see page 22)

Fruity green olive oil

½ white onion, sliced

Cucumber, radish, and scallion slices for serving

- In a food processor, grind the meat until it is creamy in texture. Grind the rose petals with a mortar and pestle and mix with 1 tablespoon of the sumac and the ginger. Mix these, some salt, and the bulgur with the meat, kneading with clean hands. Wet your hands and arrange the kibbeh mixture on an oval plate (no deeper than ½ inch/12 mm), and carve a nice checkered pattern across the top using the back of a knife.
- Drizzle the kibbeh generously with olive oil. Arrange the onion slices on top and sprinkle with some rose petals. Serve cucumber and radish slices, scallions, and sea salt on the side.

RUBY-RED BERRIES
We're used to seeing sumac as a ground spice, but it is in fact
a beautiful, bright-red berry that grows on the sumac shrub. We
have picked these berries ourselves in Turkey, in a fantastic pistachio orchard near Gaziantep. They are harvested in the fall, just
before they're ripe.

This salad is a explosion of intense flavors: exotic spices, salty sea beans, sweet-tart dressing, and pungent cheese. It's delicious with grilled meat or fish, and ideal as the greens on your Arabia buffet. Most often foraged, but now also being cultivated, sea beans (or salicornia) look like small green beans; they have a crisp, crunchy texture and a salty flavor.

Herb Salad

With sea beans, Turkish cheese, and sumac-pomegranate dressing

SERVES 6 TO 8

1 pomegranate

1 garlic clove

4 tablespoons (36 g) sumac (see page 148)

6½ tablespoons (92 ml) pomegranate molasses (see page 138)

1⅔ cups (405 ml) fruity green olive oil

½ bunch mint

1 bunch dill

1 bunch oregano

1 bunch flat-leaf parsley

1 head butter lettuce

3 ounces (75 g) arugula

1 (4-ounce/115-g) container sea beans

1¼ cups (200 g) white Turkish cheese (see page 126) or feta cheese

- Clean the pomegranate: Cut out the crown and break the pomegranate open with your thumbs. Peel the arils out and make sure the white pith doesn't come along.
- With a hand blender, puree the garlic, sumac, pomegranate molasses, and oil into a thick dressing.
- Pick the leaves from the mint, dill, oregano, and parsley and tear larger leaves into smaller pieces. Tear the lettuce leaves into smaller pieces. Mix the herbs with three-quarters of the pomegranate arils, the lettuce leaves, the arugula, and the sea beans in a large plate or bowl. Crumble the cheese on top, sprinkle with the remainder of the pomegranate arils, and drizzle some dressing on top. Serve the rest of the dressing separately so people can add to taste.

Sucuk is a popular Turkish garlic sausage, and you'll find it wrapped in plastic in the refrigerated section of Middle Eastern grocery stores. It's a dark-red, fairly firm fresh sausage that you'll need to fry first. We prefer using the whole sausage rather than presliced ones.

It's an addictively delicious, spicy sausage that goes well with nearly everything, from fried eggs to pasta sauces; it pairs especially well with lentils and chickpeas, and is a great replacement for bacon or chorizo. These semolina pizzas are simple and divine as a snack with cold beer, tart pomegranate juice, or *arak/rake* (an anise aperitif that's similar to ouzo).

Sucuk-Semolina Pizzas

With sumac and pine nuts

MAKES 15 TO 20 MINI PIZZAS

⅔ cup (100 g) semolina flour, plus extra for dusting

¾ cup (100 g) all-purpose flour, plus extra for dusting

½ cup (115 g) cold butter, cut in chunks

2 to 3 tablespoons ice-cold water

1 egg yolk

2 whole sucuk sausages

4 tablespoons (54 g) pine nuts

2 tablespoons sumac (see page 148)

- Preheat the oven to 400°F (205°C). With your hands, quickly knead the semolina with the all-purpose flour, 1 teaspoon salt, the cold butter, ice water, and egg yolk into a dough (or use a food processor). Wrap the dough in plastic wrap and let rest in the fridge. Dust the counter with flour and roll out the dough into a ¼-inch- (6-mm-) thick slab. Dust with some semolina. With a dough cutter or small drinking glass, cut out small rounds from the dough. Form another dough from the scraps, roll out, and cut more rounds. Prick small holes in them with a fork. Place on a baking sheet and bake for about 15 minutes, until golden brown.
- Meanwhile, cut the sausage into thin slices with a small, sharp knife. Heat a skillet and gently fry the sausage slices for 2 minutes. Mix with the pine nuts and let drain on paper towel. Arrange the sucuk with the pine nuts over the pizzas and sprinkle generously with sumac. Bake for another 2 minutes in the oven and serve warm.
- It's also nice to drizzle the pizzas with pomegranate molasses or sprinkle them with Aleppo pepper for an extra kick.

Intoxicating flavors

We'll never forget the souk of Damascus, with its heavy, sweet, spicy fragrances that capture the senses.

Whenever we put our nose in a container of spicy za'atar from Syria, we instantly travel back in time to the souk in Sham, Damascus. The Syrian za'atar is different from most za'atar that you'll find in the Middle East. In addition to wild thyme, sesame seed, and sumac, Syrians also add a secret mixture of spices like ground cumin, the source of that intoxicating smell. Za'atar in Lebanon, on the other hand, is made from 100 percent pure za'atar mixed with sumac and sesame seed. But what is za'atar? It is a wild thyme that resembles our oregano in taste and grows only in the Middle East. There is a round-leaf version and also one with long leaves; in the spring, you will see fresh za'atar that looks like small needles—that one is often used for pickling. Lebanese za'atar has a distinctive spicy taste, more intense than oregano: a mix of oregano and thyme. A typical breakfast in Lebanon consists of dried, ground za'atar mixed with sesame seed and sumac and baked on fresh man'ouche (Lebanese flatbread) with some olive oil. You can find Syrian za'atar and Palestinian za'atar (which is the same as the Lebanese) in some Middle Eastern grocery stores and online. Za'atar from the Maghreb is actually oregano.

Your own ras el hanout

Another one of our favorite spice mixes is Moroccan ras el hanout. What's in a name? "Head of the shop" is the translation of the name, implying a mixture of the best spices the grocer has to offer. So we allow ourselves complete liberty: This is our store! Today our ras el hanout may taste like this, tomorrow like that. We have a savory and a sweet version: the sweet one is filled with rose petals, star anise, anise, cinnamon, cardamom, and fennel seed. The quantities are somewhat arbitrary—we tend to be careful with intense spices like cumin and cardamom, but in the end it's a mixture that has to appeal to only our own taste. A bit more, a bit less—just make sure to sample occasionally. Essential is an old-fashioned coffee grinder to grind the spices, or a good, large mortar and pestle. You can buy prepared ras el hanout in Middle Eastern grocery stores, but we prefer to make it ourselves because the ones from the store always contain too much turmeric for our taste. You can use ras el hanout for chicken, lamb tajines, grilled meat, harira, kofta, couscous dishes, and sweet cakes like sfouf and sellou.

Every country its own mixture

The cuisine of every country has its own characteristic flavor enhancer. In Lebanese and Syria they use 7-spices (a mixture of allspice and various peppers) in many dishes (see recipe on page 172), and in Tunisia they use the spicy tabil, made with dry harissa, cumin, and caraway seed. Then there is the Egyptian dukkah (see recipe on page 164), a mixture of spices, nuts, and chickpeas. *Dukkah* means "to pound," and the recipe differs from family to family. You can eat dukkah with olive oil and bread for breakfast, dipping a piece of bread in the olive oil and then in the dukkah, but also as a snack and over kushari (a mixture of lentils and rice topped with pasta). In Egypt it's sold in small bags on the street. You'll find that you want to eat dukkah with everything: It's dangerously addictive—that's the magic of dukkah.

Mix and match

The entire Arab world is fond of spice mixes and each region has its own mixture: za'atar, 7-spices, and dukkah from the Middle East, ras el hanout from Morocco, and all the other *baharat* (which means "spices" in Arabic) from the Maghreb countries.

DIPS & SPICE MIXES

Besides kushari (a mixture of lentils and rice topped with pasta), dukkah is Egypt's other culinary delight. It has also been very popular for years in Australia, where many Arabs live (the second language down under is Arabic). After you've dipped your pita bread or flatbread in olive oil, it's delicious dipped in dukkah. Soon you'll discover that it's delicious with everything: in salads, over vegetables and soups, over labneh. Be careful, though: A friend of ours once bought regular chickpeas instead of roasted, and ended up with a stomachache!

This is our dukkah for today; tomorrow it could be all different. You can replace oregano with dried mint.

Arabia's Dukkah

SERVES 8 TO 10

1 cup (200 g) roasted, dried chickpeas (see page 82)

3 cups (300 g) roasted almonds

⅔ cup (100 g) raw sesame seeds, plus 3 tablespoons more for garnish

5 tablespoons coriander seed

2 tablespoons cumin seed

3 tablespoons anise seed

2 tablespoons fennel seed

2 tablespoons dried oregano

2 tablespoons dried edible rose petals (available at baking supply shops and online)

2 tablespoons grated orange zest

Fruty green olive oil, for serving

Arabic bread, for serving

- Preheat the oven to 350°F (175°C). Spread the chickpeas, almonds, sesame seeds (except for the garnish), the coriander, cumin, anise, and fennel seeds, and the oregano on a rimmed baking sheet. Bake for about 8 minutes (tossing halfway through the baking time), until the spices and nuts become fragrant.
- Grind the roasted ingredients to a fine texture in a food processor (or grind with a big mortar and pestle if you feel like doing it by hand). After grinding, stir in the remaining 3 tablespoons sesame seeds.
- Serve in a pretty pile sprinkled with the rose petals and orange zest, with a bowl of fruity green olive oil and Arabic bread. Dip your bread first in olive oil and then in the dukkah. You can also add sliced tomatoes and cucumbers, sprigs of mint, and olives for a big breakfast, lunch, or a snack!

We came across all kinds of hummus throughout the Middle East. These dips
are not only delicious and healthy; they're also easy to make and a feast for the eye.
Serve them with flatbread or another nice bread of your choice.

Hummus

EACH SERVES 4 TO 6;
COMBINED,
THEY SERVE 8 TO 12

CARROT HUMMUS
14 ounces (400 g) carrots
½ clove garlic
²/3 cup (165 ml) white tahini
    (see page 58)
Lemon juice
Fruity green olive oil
Aleppo pepper (see page 44)

FAVA BEAN HUMMUS
1¼ pounds (500 g) shelled
    fava beans
½ clove garlic
²/3 cup (165 ml) white tahini
    (see page 58)
Lemon juice
Fruity green olive oil
Ground cumin
Aleppo pepper (see page 44)

BEET HUMMUS
14 ounces (400 g) raw beets
½ clove garlic
²/3 cup (165 ml) white tahini
    (see page 58)
Lemon juice
Fruity green olive oil
Sumac (see page 148)

· CARROT HUMMUS

Boil or steam the carrots for about 15 minutes. Drain and let cool. With
a hand blender, puree the carrots with the garlic and tahini. Season with
salt and lemon juice. Scoop onto a plate, drizzle generously with olive oil,
and sprinkle with some Aleppo pepper.

· FAVA BEAN HUMMUS

Boil or steam the beans for about 10 minutes. Drain and let cool. With a
hand blender, puree the beans with the garlic and tahini. Season with salt
and lemon juice. Scoop onto a plate, drizzle generously with olive oil, and
sprinkle with some cumin and Aleppo pepper.

· BEET HUMMUS

Boil the beets for about 45 minutes. Drain and cool, then peel. With a
hand blender, puree the beets with the garlic and tahini. Season with salt
and lemon juice. Scoop onto a plate, drizzle generously with olive oil, and
sprinkle with some sumac.

Here's another of our addictions: za'atar (or za'tar), a mixture of local wild thyme (which looks and tastes like oregano, but with a more intense flavor), sesame seeds, and sumac. Za'atar is the name of both the herb itself and the spice mixture. To make things even more confusing, both the mixture and the herb are often called green thyme or oregano. The mixture za'atar is eaten in Lebanon, Jordan, and Syria. It's usually mixed with olive oil and baked on Lebanese man'ouche, the flatbread that's eaten for breakfast. In Syria, they like to mix it with spices like cumin. We have added finely ground rose petals to our za'atar, which makes it even more special. The flavor makes us daydream of our beloved Middle East. You can buy za'atar in Middle Eastern grocery stores or online.

Za'atar

With rose petals

SERVES 8 TO 10

4 tablespoons (24 g) dried edible rose petals (available at baking supply shops and online)

8 tablespoons (48 g) Za'atar

Fruity green olive oil, for serving

Flatbread, for serving

- Grind the rose petals to a fine powder with a mortar and pestle and mix with some sea salt and the za'atar.
- Serve with small bowls of olive oil and flatbread. Dip your bread first in the olive and then in the Za'atar.

Ras el hanout is a spice mixture from the spice shop. The name means "head of the shop," or the shop's best spices. Simply put, because your kitchen is your shop, you can make your own mixture. Constant tasting ensures that you'll find the ideal combination. We like to use sweet ras el hanout for cookies and sfouf (almond-semolina cake), olive oil cake (page 18), and sellou (page 78). The savory version is delicious in meat and vegetable stews, with chicken, couscous, harira (Moroccan soup), and b'stilla (page 178). Grains of paradise are dark-brown grains with a distinctive flavor; you can buy them at spice shops and online. You can also leave them out. If you can't find Tellicherry pepper or long pepper, replace with regular black pepper. It's best to use whole spices that are as fresh as possible, and grind them yourself. A mortar and pestle or small electric coffee grinder is essential.

Ras el Hanout

Sweet and Savory

MAKES ABOUT
½ CUP (60g) EACH

SWEET RAS EL HANOUT
2 tablespoons cumin seed
1 tablespoon fennel seed
1 tablespoon anise seed
1 tablespoon cinnamon or 1 broken cinnamon stick
1 star anise
½ tablespoon grains of paradise
2 teaspoons white peppercorns
½ tablespoon Tellicherry or long peppercorns (or black peppercorns)
1 tablespoon coriander seed
1 tablespoon dried edible rose petals (available at baking supply shops and online)

SAVORY RAS EL HANOUT
2 tablespoons cumin seed
2 tablespoons coriander seed
½ tablespoon cinnamon or 1 broken cinnamon stick
1 star anise
½ tablespoon grains of paradise
1 tablespoon whole cloves
1 tablespoon ground ginger
1 teaspoon saffron threads
½ tablespoon Tellicherry or long pepper peppercorns (or black peppercorns)

• SWEET RAS EL HANOUT

Heat a dry skillet and toast the cumin, fennel, and anise seeds, the cinnamon, star anise, grains of paradise, peppercorns, and coriander seed for 1 minute. Finely grind all the spices and the rose petals in a mortar and pestle or a coffee grinder. Store in a closed container in a cool, dark place.

• SAVORY RAS EL HANOUT

Heat a dry skillet and toast the cumin and coriander seeds, cinnamon, star anise, grains of paradise, cloves, ginger, saffron, and peppercorns for 1 minute. Finely grind all the spices in a mortar and pestle or a coffee grinder. Store in a closed container in a cool, dark place.

It's not a Lebanese household without 7-spices. You can buy it prepared, but homemade is always better. You'll actually find 7-spices all over the Middle East, and it gives many dishes their distinctive flavor, especially because of the allspice and cinnamon. Everyone has their own version. Note that this mixture is not comparable to ras el hanout.

Seven-spices is essential in kibbeh, kibbey nayeh (page 154), and other Middle Eastern dishes like maqlooba (page 130) and the herbed rice salad with 7-spices dressing (page 236).

Sabaa Baharat

7-spices

MAKES ABOUT ½ CUP
(60g)

1 tablespoon black pepper-corns

2 tablespoons allspice

2 tablespoons ground cinna-mon

1 tablespoon whole cloves

1 tablespoon coriander seed

½ tablespoon ground ginger

1 teaspoon freshly ground nutmeg

• Heat a dry skillet and toast the peppercorns, allspice, cinnamon, cloves, coriander seed, ginger, and nutmeg for 1 minute. Grind the spices in a mortar and pestle or electric coffee grinder. Store in a closed container in a cool, dark place.

On dates and figs

Dates are widely available in different qualities: Look for
the Tunisian and Algerian deglet nour in Middle Eastern groceries. Packaged
dried figs are usually sold with a bay leaf to keep the flies away. Figs, apricots,
and dates are delicious with herb tea (or dipped in tahini—yum!), but
we also like to use them in salads, stews, desserts, and shakes or drinks.
Serving your guests bowls of dried fruits is a sign of hospitality. Dried fruits
keep for a long time, but always check them for small insects.

Mish mish

Pretty yellow apricots
(*mish mish*) are treated
with sulfites to prevent
discoloring—they'd
become black otherwise.
Egyptians like an apricot
drink made from the dried
sheets of apricot puree
that you'll find in Middle
Eastern grocery stores.
They dissolve the sheets in
hot water and add sugar.

Date palm climbers

Dates come in different varieties
and you'll find them most often from
Tunisia, Egypt, Algeria, Iran, and Israel. Deglet nour is a very lovely, fleshy
date that's not too sweet. We have eaten
them directly from the tree in Tolga, in
the Biskra of Algeria. The trees can grow
to more than 80 feet high. Men with
ropes around their middle climb quickly
up the tree and come down heavy-laden
with dates. Dates that ripen on the tree are
the best quality. Other dates are picked when
they're unripe. The large, soft medjool dates
are very sweet and often come from Israel.
Dates contain more fructose than any other
fruit and are filled with antioxidants, minerals,
and vitamins. The Tuareg bedouins feed their
women camel's milk with dates so they become
beautifully curvy; we saw this with our own eyes
in the desert of Libya.

How ripe are dates?

In the fall, you'll find yellow, unripe dates in Middle Eastern stores. They are tangy, rough, and a bit sour. There are different names for the various degrees of ripeness: kimri (unripe), khalal (crunchy and ripe), rutab (soft and ripe), and tamr and tamar (ripe and dried).

Fig wreath

Dried figs are a true delicacy: less sweet than dates and with a lot of flavor and structure. Figs exist in purple and green varieties; the green are often more more fleshy and juicy, and they are most often used to make dried figs. The quality differs. We are very fond of the amazing, mouth-watering, dried fig wreath from the organic market Souk el Tayeb in Beirut. But Italian figs with anise seed from Fichi Secchidi Carmignano are also divine. The combination of figs and anise is really lovely; there is also a terrific fig marmalade with sesame and anise seeds from the Middle East that you'll sometimes see in stores. Figs are a good source of calcium.

FIGS, DATES & APRICOTS

Dating

Our friend and designer (see the lovely pomegranate napkins on page 103) Marije Vogelzang organized a great project with dates—Project Blind Date—at the Virginia Commonwealth University extension in Qatar. Because dating is prohibited in strict Islamic countries like Qatar, Marije gave blindfolded participants (both men and women) their first introduction through a sampling of various dates that differed in color, texture, and taste. It was the first step in choosing their ideal date!

Nearly all Arabic countries have a dessert or cookie based on toasted flour, like sfouf (an almond-semolina cake) and sellou (see page 78). From Bahrain comes afoosa: toasted flour mixed with date paste made from soft dates. You can buy it prepared, or you can make it yourself. We add saffron and cardamom to make it even more exciting. The texture is similar to fudge and is lovely served with mascarpone and some saffron tea.

Date-Saffron Fudge

SERVES 8 TO 10

1½ cups (200 g) all-purpose flour

⅓ cup (50 g) raw sesame seeds

7 ounces (200 g) pitted, soft dates or date paste

¾ cup (180 ml) fruity green olive oil

¼ teaspoon cardamom

Pinch of saffron threads

- Preheat the oven to 400°F (205°C). Cover a baking sheet with parchment paper and spread the flour and sesame seeds evenly over it. Toast the mixture in the oven for a few minutes, stirring regularly with a wooden spoon, until golden brown. Don't walk away, because it can burn very quickly! Remove from the oven and transfer to a large saucepan.
- Pulse the dates into a smooth paste in a food processor, if not using prepared date paste. Heat the flour-sesame mixture over low heat and, while stirring, slowly add the olive oil. Once the oil is absorbed, add the date paste, cardamom, and saffron and keep stirring until the mixture forms a dough ball and comes loose from the bottom. Divide the warm afoosa onto serving plates.

This is a classic dish of Moroccan cuisine. It's a very festive dish—in fact, everyone eats it from one plate. This version is extra special because it's filled with date and orange-zest sugar, instead of the more common cinnamon sugar. We've replaced the traditional pigeon with chicken.

B'stilla

With saffron chicken, almonds, dates, and orange-zest sugar

SERVES 6

3 small onions

½ bunch flat-leaf parsley

½ bunch cilantro

2½ pounds (1 kg) chicken thighs

Mild olive oil

3 tablespoons savory ras el hanout (purchased or home-made, see page 170)

1 teaspoon ground fenugreek

2 pinches saffron

1 cup (100 g) blanched almonds

3½ ounces (100 g) pitted dates

2 large eggs

½ cup (115 g) butter

About 6 large sheets phyllo dough (do not use frozen, see page 202)

6 tablespoons (75 g) sugar

Grated zest of 1 orange

- Finely chop the onions, parsley, and ci-lantro and set aside. Season the chicken legs with salt and pepper. Heat a gener-ous amount of olive oil in a Dutch oven and fry the chicken until golden brown. Take the chicken out and sauté the on-ions in the same pan for 10 minutes. Add the parsley and the cilantro, the ras el hanout, fenugreek, and saffron and sauté for 1 minute. Put the chicken legs back in the pan, add 1¼ cups (300 ml) water and cover the pan. Let them braise for about 1½ hours over low heat, until tender. Flip the chicken regularly.

- In a skillet, fry the almonds in some olive oil over medium heat until golden brown, about 5 minutes. Let drain on a paper towel. Finely chop the almonds and dates and set aside in a bowl.

- Take the chicken out of the pan and let it cool. Beat the eggs and carefully stir them into the sauce that's left in the pan. Continue to stir and let thicken for 3 minutes on low heat. Allow to cool.

- Preheat the oven to 400°F (205°C). Pull the chicken meat from the bones (discard the skin). Mix the chicken with the sauce. Melt the butter. Line a baking dish (a 10-inch/25-cm pie plate works perfectly) with three sheets of buttered phyllo dough; make sure the entire bot-tom and sides are covered, with plenty of overhang. Spoon the chicken with the sauce into the covered form, and divide the almond-date mixture on top. Fold the phyllo dough toward the middle to cover the filling. Butter a few more phyllo dough sheets, form into a round shape, and use them to nicely wrap the entire b'stilla.

- Bake in the middle of the oven for about 30 minutes, until golden brown and crispy. Grind the sugar with the orange zest and sprinkle liberally over the b'stilla. Slice and serve straight from the baking dish.

Bukra fi mish mish—Tomorrow there will be apricots (meaning tomorrow will bring sunshine or tomorrow all your wishes will come true).

—Arabic proverb

We first saw this beautiful fig wreath at the Souk el Tayeb, the organic farmer's market in Beirut. It was made by the Druze, a small, mystical religious community that has followers in Lebanon, Syria, Israel, and Jordan (followers are recognized by the beautiful white veils worn by both men and women, with characteristic black pants). Because we don't always have access to these delicious fig wreaths—made from beautiful, dried pale figs—we make them ourselves and then dip them in tahini. Irresistible!

Fig Wreath

With anise seed and tahini dip

MAKES 1 LARGE FIG
WREATH

2½ pounds (1 kg) dried figs

A few bay leaves

3 tablespoons anise seed

White tahini (see page 58)

- Tear the figs open and flatten them. Using a large plate or cake stand as your guide, create a nice, not-too-large circle of figs around the edge. Place the first layer of figs on the plate, open side up. Press in a bay leaf occasionally and sprinkle with some anise seed. Press another layer of figs on top and repeat until the last layer (when you've run out of figs), which should have the figs facing down. Place a large, heavy plate on top and let the figs sit for a few days in a cool, dry spot.

- When ready to serve, whip the tahini in a small bowl and serve alongside the fig wreath for dipping. This is delicious with a cup of strong Arabic or Turkish coffee or a cup of herb tea. Wrapped in plastic, the fig wreath will keep for a few weeks.

This really is a lovely, festive dish—a simple rustic chicken made chic by dried Mediterranean fruits, delicious nuts, and, of course, our homemade ras el hanout. The vermicelli filling is a classic.

Chicken with Preserved Lemon

With ras el hanout and date-apricot vermicelli

SERVES 4

1 preserved lemon (see page 34)

1 (2- to 3-pound/910-g to 1½-kg) organic chicken

4 tablespoons (36 g) savory ras el hanout (see page 170)

Mild olive oil

1 (1-pound/500-g) bag short vermicelli (found in Middle Eastern grocery stores)

8 pitted dates

8 dried apricots

¾ cup (75 g) almonds

6 tablespoons (36 g) finely chopped flat-leaf parsley or cilantro

- Quarter the preserved lemon, scoop out the soft flesh, and slice the zest in very fine strips. Rub the chicken thoroughly with half of the zest, the ras el hanout, ample salt and pepper, and a generous splash of olive oil. Massage the ras el hanout mixture into the chicken and allow the chicken to marinate for at least 30 minutes or up to a few hours in a snug baking dish in the fridge.
- Preheat the oven to 500°F (260°C). Roast the chicken for about 15 minutes, until golden brown all over. Lower the heat to 300°F (150°C) and roast the chicken for another 45 minutes, until tender. Insert a small knife between breast and leg, and if the juices run clear, the chicken is ready; if not, roast for another 15 to 20 minutes.
- Bring ample water to a boil in the bottom pan of a couscoussière. If you don't have a couscoussière, use a large, deep metal strainer set inside a pot with water in the bottom; don't let the water touch the strainer. Wrap the pot lid in a towel if it doesn't fit snugly over the strainer, to prevent too much steam from escaping. Put the vermicelli in a large bowl and mix with 3 tablespoons olive oil and a pinch of salt. Sprinkle with half a glass of cold water and stir well, rubbing the vermicelli with your hands. Put the vermicelli in the top compartment of the couscoussière and steam for 10 minutes.
- Thinly slice the dates and apricots. Coarsely chop the almonds. Scoop the steamed vermicelli into a large bowl, allow to cool a little, and sprinkle again with some water. Mix the dates, apricots, almonds, and the remaining lemon zest with the vermicelli; add 1 tablespoon olive oil if needed (if the vermicelli are sticking together). Put the vermicelli back in the couscoussière and steam for another 8 minutes.
- To finish, mix the vermicelli with some of the spicy chicken drippings from the baking dish and the parsley. Scoop some of the vermicelli into the chicken cavity and serve the chicken on top of the rest.

The entire Moroccan tajine culture is often reduced to just two dishes: tajine with chicken, green olives, and preserved lemon and tajine with lamb, almonds, and prunes. But there are endless combinations possible, as proven by this simple lamb tajine with figs, potatoes, cinnamon, and rosemary. It's delicious in every season.

Lamb Tajine

With figs, cinnamon, and rosemary

SERVES 4

2 red onions

Mild olive oil

1 teaspoon ground cardamom

1 cinnamon stick

2½ pounds (1 kg) lamb shoulder, in chunks

4 large Yukon gold potatoes

8 dried figs

3 sprigs rosemary

- Cut the onions into wedges. Heat some olive oil in a tajine or cast-iron Dutch oven and sauté the onions with the cardamom, cinnamon stick, and the lamb for about 15 minutes, until golden brown.
- Cut the potatoes (do not peel) into wedges and halve the figs. Add the potatoes, a pinch of salt, and the figs to the pan. Add enough water to cover. Strip the rosemary leaves from the stems, finely chop most of the leaves (save a few for garnish), and add to the pan.
- Stew the lamb tajine over low heat for about 40 minutes, until tender; season with salt and pepper. Garnish with the remaining rosemary leaves.

Buying pasta

Middle Eastern grocery
stores sell all kinds of
different small pastas.
Become inspired and mix
it up. Put them in soups
or serve with a thick
spicy sauce for a real
Arabian pasta dish.

With yogurt

In Morocco and the Middle
East you often see a kind
of broken vermicelli eaten
as a pasta, and also in
combination with rice or
legumes. Short, couscous-
like pasta can be found on
Sardinia (fregula) and in
Lebanon (moghrabieh).
Turks also love their short
pastas, and you can find
them in Turkish shops in
all sizes and shapes. Turks
like their pasta with yogurt.
Afghans and Lebanese also
love pasta with yogurt: as
mantior shish barak (meat-
filled pasta in a warm yogurt
sauce, see page 264).

In the sauce

Like the Italians, the Arabians have always loved eating pasta. The one big difference between the Italian and the Arabian traditions is the manner in which the pasta is cooked: not in water, but in the sauce. This way the sauce infuses the pasta with flavor. Short pasta like riso is often put in hearty, main-course soups (*chorba*) in Maghreb countries like Morocco and Tunisia.

PASTA

In the Sicilian pesto Trapanese (a pesto made from almonds, tomato, garlic, and fresh basil), the Arabian influences can be seen in both the ingredients and the use of the mortar and pestle. There are also similarities with the Catalan picada—also a remnant of Arabian culture, here from the Moors. We mixed half of the pesto with the minced meat, creating a kind of köfte and making the pasta even more Arabian (yet very acceptable for Italians).

Pappardelle
With köfte and pesto Trapanese

SERVES 4

1 cup (100 g) almonds

1 bunch basil

1 clove garlic

3 tablespoons tomato paste, divided

Fruity green olive oil

12 ounces (350 g) ground lamb

Mild olive oil

1 shallot

14 ounces (400 g) pappardelle

- Using a hand blender, process the almonds, basil, and garlic with 1 tablespoon of the tomato paste and ⅔ cup (165 ml) oil (you can also use a large mortar and pestle). Season with a pinch of salt. Mix about 6 tablespoons (90 ml) of the pesto with the ground lamb and form cigarlike köftes. Heat some oil in a skillet and fry the köftes over medium heat, turning with a spatula, until browned and cooked through. Cover to keep the köftes warm while you make the pasta.

- Heat a generous amount of oil in a skillet. Mince the shallot and sauté until light brown. Add the rest of the tomato paste and cook gently for another 10 minutes on low heat. Season with salt. Meanwhile, boil the pasta in ample water with some salt until al dente, following the cooking instructions on the package.

- Drain the pasta and place in a bowl. Fold in the rest of the pesto and the tomato-shallot oil. Serve with the köftes.

Sucuk, the dried Turkish garlic sausage, is a good friend of the fried egg. This is comfort food infused with Turkish flavors, especially through the use of large amounts of fresh dill.

Turkish Pasta

With sucuk, chickpeas, and dill

SERVES 4

1 cup (200 g) chickpeas (soaked overnight, see page 82)

10½ ounces (300 g) riso (or bird tongue) pasta (available at Middle Eastern grocery stores, see page 188)

2 sucuk sausages (available at Middle Eastern grocery stores)

4 large eggs

Mild olive oil

1 bunch dill

1 clove garlic

Fruity green olive oil

- Cook the chickpeas in ample water for about 45 minutes, until tender. Drain and set aside. Following the cooking instructions on the package, cook the pasta until al dente. Peel the casing off the sausages and slice them. Heat a large skillet and fry the sucuk until golden brown, about 10 minutes. Remove and drain on paper towels.
- Using the same pan, fry the eggs on low heat (add a splash of mild olive oil, if needed). Mince the dill.
- Remove the eggs from the pan. Drain the pasta and mix with the chickpeas, sucuk, garlic, half of the dill, a splash of fruity green olive oil, and some salt. Serve the pasta with the fried eggs on top and sprinkle with the rest of the dill.

A PLATE OF ARABIAN PASTA

We once read somewhere that the history of pasta is as complicated as a plate filled with spaghetti; that's a nice comparison. Most likely it was the Arabs who introduced pasta to Italy by way of Palermo, the capital of Sicily. It was, after all, the Arabs who brought hard wheat (also called durum wheat or macaroni wheat) from northern Africa. After the tomato arrived from the New World, the Italians came up with the idea of tomato sauce. Coincidentally, this made the use of the fork necessary; until that time people had been eating pasta with their hands.

An Arabia pasta salad inspired by southern Italy, in which the riso functions as rice (*riso* in Italian). Deep-frying the capers not only makes them crunchy, but also makes their flavor bloom.

Riso Salad

With asparagus, lemon, ricotta, and buffalo mozzarella

SERVES 4 TO 6

1 fennel bulb

1 bunch green asparagus

1 bunch scallions

1 bunch basil

14 ounces (400 g) riso (or bird tongue) pasta (available at Middle Eastern grocery stores, see page 188)

Mild olive oil

3 tablespoons salted capers

1 (7-ounce/200-g) buffalo mozzarella

¾ cup (180 ml) fruity green olive oil

Grated zest and juice of 1 lemon

½ (12-ounce/340-g) container fresh ricotta cheese

- Finely chop the fennel. Blanch the asparagus for 5 minutes, rinse, and thinly slice. Mince the scallion. Pick the basil leaves and tear into small pieces.
- Cook the pasta until al dente according to the package directions.
- Heat a good amount of mild olive oil in a skillet and deep-fry the capers for about 3 minutes, until golden brown and crunchy. Drain on paper towels.
- Shred the mozzarella into small strings. Make a dressing from the fruity green olive oil, 2 tablespoons lemon juice, the lemon zest, and some salt.
- Mix the riso with the fennel, asparagus, scallion, basil, and one-half of the dressing; arrange in a large dish. Spoon the ricotta in dots over the salad and sprinkle the mozzarella on top. Drizzle with the remaining half of the dressing and garnish with the fried capers.

This is a Spanish-Arabian pasta. You can use vermicelli from the Middle Eastern grocery store, but you can also break spaghetti into pieces. *Pimentón* is a typically Spanish seasoning. It's a sweet smoked paprika found in spice shops or online. You can also replace it with sweet paprika. *Mígas* is a kind of poor man's Parmesan, made from old bread.

Fideus

With grilled squid and migas

SERVES 4

3 onions

4 cloves garlic, divided

Mild olive oil

1 (14-ounce/400-g) can peeled tomatoes

4 tablespoons (60 g) Turkish paprika paste (see page 44)

2½ tablespoons (60 g) pimentón or sweet paprika, divided

10½ ounces (300 g) vermicelli

½ pan bread (see page 251) or other rustic bread (about 8 ounces/220g)

14 ounces (400 g) squid, cleaned

½ bunch flat-leaf parsley

- Coarsely chop the onions and 3 of the garlic cloves. Heat a generous splash of oil in a large saucepan and sauté the onions and the garlic for about 10 minutes over low heat. Add the (mildly crushed) peeled tomatoes, the paprika paste, 2 tablespoons of the pimentón, a tiny pinch of salt (the paprika paste already is quite salty), and some freshly ground black pepper and bring to a boil. Add a good amount of boiling water and blend the vermicelli with the sauce (there has to be enough sauce for the vermicelli to cook in). If the mixture gets too dry during cooking, add some more water. Cook until the pasta is al dente, about 8 minutes.
- Prepare the migas (bread crumbs) by crumbling the bread into small pieces. Mince the remaining garlic clove. Fry the bread crumbs and garlic to a crisp in a skillet with a tiny splash of oil. Season with some salt and the remaining pimentón.
- Meanwhile, heat a grill pan. Open the squid with a knife and, over high heat, briefly grill them on both sides. Mince the parsley and blend with the grilled squid, some oil, and some salt. Serve the pasta with the squid and sprinkle with the migas.

This is a quintessential Arabia recipe: It isn't Turkish, it isn't Italian—it's a pasta using exclusively Middle Eastern ingredients. Although our Middle Eastern friends wouldn't necessarily prepare it like this, we'd like to cook it for them because we're sure they'll like it just as much as we do. It may seem a bit complicated to prepare all the flavorings separately, but it's not difficult and it's definitely worth the effort.

Short Turkish Pasta

With pulled lemon-garlic chicken, tahini, and yogurt

SERVES 4

4 cloves garlic

4 chicken thighs

Mild olive oil

Grated zest of 2 lemons

2 cups (500 g) full-fat Turkish or Greek yogurt (see page 126)

1 teaspoon cornstarch

10½ ounces (300 g) short-cut Turkish pasta (available at Middle Eastern groceries)

3 shallots

14 ounces (400 g) chard or spinach

¾ cup (75 g) natural (unblanched) almonds

¾ cup (180 ml) white tahini (see page 58)

Fruity green olive oil

- Preheat the oven to 350°F (175°C). Grate or mince the garlic. Rub the chicken with some mild olive oil, the lemon zest, half of the garlic, and some salt. Roast the chicken for about 50 minutes. Remove the chicken from the oven but leave the oven on. Let the chicken cool pull the meat from the bones (discard the skin).

- Over low heat, whisk the yogurt with the rest of the garlic and the cornstarch; do not let it boil. Season with salt to taste. Following the cooking instructions on the package, cook the pasta until al dente. Slice the shallots lengthwise and stir-fry with the chard in some olive oil for about 10 minutes. Roast the almonds until golden brown in the oven. Let them cool, then chop coarsely. Pour some boiling water into the tahini and stir until you get a nice, smooth sauce. Season with salt.

- Combine the pasta with the chicken and the chard and generously ladle the yogurt sauce and the tahini sauce over everything. Sprinkle with almonds and drizzle with some fruity green oil.

Working with phyllo dough

Before using, always lightly brush both sides of a phyllo dough sheet with melted butter or oil. Some sheets of phyllo dough are extremely thin and tear easily, so try out various brands. The best-quality dough comes from Middle Eastern stores. Take the dough from the refrigerator or the shelves; if possible.
We prefer the ones sold in long plastic rolls. Most phyllo dough from regular supermarkets is too small and dry; we suggest looking in specialty Middle Eastern grocery stores, for larger, less try, slightly thicker phyllo. It's important to work fast and to store any dough you're not immediately using under a clean kitchen towel to keep it from drying out.

Yufka dough comes in both large square and triangular sheets. It's slightly thicker than phyllo dough but still pretty delicate. We used the triangular sheets for our delicious yufka rolls (page 212). You'll find yufka sheets on the shelves in Middle Eastern grocery stores. Beware: Yufka and phyllo dough are often confused with each other. Ask if you're unsure which is which.

PHYLLO & YUFKA DOUGH

In Turkish, Balkan, and Middle Eastern cuisines (not to mention Greek), a life without phyllo dough is unimaginable. Phyllo dough is used in both savory and sweet dishes (baklava, for instance). Yufka dough is used only for savory recipes. The dough is unleavened and is made from just flour and water. The Moroccan ouar dough, which is needed for making real b'stilla, can be replaced by phyllo dough without any problem. Briq dough, mainly used in Tunisian cuisine, has a structure similar to spring roll wrappers, but they're round instead of square. They're difficult to find, and spring roll wrappers are a good alternative.

At Moroccan weddings a towering m'hancha (or rolled up snake) is often served as the showpiece of the dinner table. We have tried the filling using nuts alone and also with sweet dried Mediterranean fruits. These m'hanchas are easy to make because we keep our rolled-up snakes to a modest size. These are delicious plain, but also great with unsweetened clotted cream, mascarpone, or creamy Turkish yogurt, as well as strong Moroccan mint tea.

M'hancha

With dried Mediterranean fruits and cinnamon sugar

SERVES 8 TO 12

5¼ ounces (150 g) pitted dates

5¼ ounces (150 g) dried figs

5¼ ounces (150 g) dried apricots

1 cup (150 g) dried cranberries

1 cup (100 g) salted roasted almonds

1 cup (100 g) walnuts

2 to 3 tablespoons walnut or almond oil

1 roll phyllo dough (preferably fresh, see page 202)

½ cup (115 g) butter, melted

1 egg yolk, beaten

2 tablespoons cinnamon

3 tablespoons sugar

- Coarsely chop the dates, figs, apricots, and cranberries, then grind them in a food processor together with the nuts until you get a chunky paste. If needed, add some nut oil to create a homogenous paste.
- Wrap the sheets of phyllo dough in a clean kitchen towel and remove one sheet at a time just when you are about to use it. Line a baking sheet with parchment paper. Shape the fruit nut paste into "fingers" about ¾ inch (2 cm) thick.
- Preheat the oven to 400°F (205°C). Place a sheet of phyllo dough lengthwise in front of you on the counter. Generously brush with melted butter and place a "fruits-and-nuts finger" about ¾ inch (2 cm) from the edge. Making sure the filling stays inside, roll up the dough over the filling until you get a long thin roll. Carefully lift the first roll and place it at the center of the baking sheet. Bend it into a tightly wound spiral. Bend it gently, otherwise the dough will rip. Repeat with the rest of the dough sheets and "fingers."
- Brush the m'hancha with some egg yolk. Mix the cinnamon with the sugar and sprinkle over the m'hancha. Bake for about 15 minutes, until golden brown and crispy. Allow the m'hancha to cool before serving or eat while they're still warm.

An elegant twist on the Moroccan sweet *b'stilla au lait* (thin, crêpe-like layers filled with custard). The orange blossom custard in the b'stilla resembles the Lebanese milk pudding mhallabieh. The delightful, fresh, sweet-tart orange Japanese medlars, which are only briefly in season in the spring, make this a wonderful dessert pastry. You can buy medlars (also known loquats, Japanese plums, or mzehh) at Middle Eastern grocery stores or large Asian markets.

Phyllo Dough Pastries
With mhallabieh and medlars

SERVES 2

2 cups (480 ml) whole milk

2 tablespoons sugar

2 heaping tablespoons cornstarch

Orange blossom water

4 large sheets phyllo dough (preferably fresh, see page 202)

½ cup (115 g) melted butter

8 ripe Japanese medlars (loquats)

1 tablespoon lemon juice

1 tablespoon honey

4 tablespoons (25 g) sweet-salty nuts (page 226)

- In a saucepan over low heat, warm the milk with the sugar, stirring until all sugar has dissolved. Add a splash of cold water to the cornstarch, stir to make a slurry, and add to the milk. Stir continuously over medium heat until the custard begins to boil, then lower the heat, but continue to stir until the custard slowly trickles from a wooden spoon. Strain through a fine-mesh sieve and add 1 to 2 tablespoons orange blossom water, to taste. Continue to stir until the custard has cooled off and becomes somewhat clotted. Keep in a cool place until ready to use, but not in the fridge or the custard will become too solid.

- Preheat the oven to 400°F (205°C). Using a dough cutter or a sharp-edged glass, cut 20 identical circles from the phyllo dough and lightly butter both sides. Line a baking sheet with parchment and make 4 stacks of 5 buttered sheets each. Bake these a few minutes, until golden brown and crispy. Remove from the oven and set aside to cool.

- Peel the medlars, cut them in half, and remove the pits. Cut into wedges and combine with the lemon juice and honey. Finely chop the nuts.

- Divide the custard over 2 phyllo stacks, place another 2 stacks on top of them, and again spoon a generous amount of custard over them. Garnish with some medlar wedges and sprinkle with the nuts. Serve the remaining custard, medlars, and nuts separately as extra topping.

A super easy snack made from crisp phyllo dough, some adventurous cheese, and fragrant oregano. Great with cold beer, arak (an anise-flavored Middle Eastern alcoholic drink), or wine. When they're in season (in early spring), serve with some fresh green, crispy almonds. Don't substitute feta cheese for tulum; it is not the right texture. Look for tulum in Middle Eastern grocery stores, or purchase online.

Börek

With nomad cheese and oregano

SERVES 6 TO 8

1 clove garlic

2 sprigs oregano

⅓ cup (84 g) tulum (dry Turkish nomad cheese, see page 126)

2 large sheets phyllo dough (or large yufka sheets, see page 202)

Mild olive oil

- Preheat the oven to 400°F (205°C).
- Mince the garlic; strip the leaves from the oregano stems and mince these as well. Combine the cheese with the garlic and the oregano.
- Lightly brush a large phyllo dough sheet with some oil and fold width-wise. Place on a baking sheet lined with parchment paper. Sprinkle the cheese mixture in a thin, even layer on top of the folded dough sheet. Lightly brush the second sheet of phyllo with some oil as well; fold and place on top of the cheese-sprinkled sheet. Using a fork, pierce the phyllo dough in a couple of places. With a sharp knife, cut the dough into 6 even squares, and then diagonally cut the squares into 4 triangles each.
- Bake in the hot oven for about 10 minutes, until golden brown and crispy.

We don't like to brag, but fish b'stillas this good are a rare treat. Most fish b'stilla tend to be dry, but this fish filling stays moist because we briefly cook the fish in a rich saffron-fennel sauce, separate from the other ingredients. Don't be afraid to rip the phyllo sheets when folding them; just use an extra oiled sheet to wrap your wonderful, delicate, and round b'stillas once more.

Fish B'stilla

With sautéed saffron fennel and fennel salad

SERVES 4

3 onions

2 large fennel bulbs

Mild olive oil

3 pinches saffron

⅓ cup (50 g) raisins

2 tablespoons fennel seed

10½ ounces (300 g) hake, cod, or haddock filet

8 sheets phyllo dough (do not use frozen, see page 202)

½ cups (115 g) butter, melted

2 oranges

4 tablespoons (45 g) pomegranate arils

- Cube the onions and the fennel; reserve the fennel fronds. Heat a good amount of oil in a pan and sauté the fennel and onion cubes for 5 minutes over medium heat. Add the saffron, raisins, fennel seed, some salt, and a generous amount of freshly ground black pepper. Simmer for 25 minutes over low heat.
- Slice the fish into chunks, add them to the saffron-fennel mixture, and cook for 5 minutes. Remove from the heat and let cool slightly. Meanwhile, preheat the oven to 400°F (205°C).
- Place a sheet of phyllo dough lengthwise in front of you on the counter. Generously brush with melted butter and place one-quarter of the fish-saffron mixture at the center of the sheet. Fold the phyllo around the filling as neatly as possible. Then butter another sheet of dough and gently fold it around the just-wrapped b'stilla. While folding, try to create a nice round shape. Using the same method, create the other 3 b'stillas. Carefully place them on a parchment paper–lined baking sheet and bake for about 10 minutes, until golden brown.
- Thinly slice the rest of the fennel. Peel the oranges, removing all the pith. Holding them over a bowl to collect the juice, cut the orange wedges loose from their membranes. Mix the fennel slices with the orange juice, orange wedges, fennel leaves, and pomegranate arils. Serve with some of the fennel salad. A lemon wedge is also nice to squeeze over your salad and b'stilla.

We first published a recipe for our yufka rolls in our book *Bismilla Arabia*. They proved to be so popular, we couldn't resist making a new, even more fragrant version. Za'atar is mixed with ground lamb and a warm garlic–pine nut butter for spooning over the cold yogurt.

Yufka Rolls

With za'atar, cold yogurt, and warm garlic–pine nut butter

SERVES 4

1 red onion

10½ ounces (300 g) ground lamb

4 tablespoons (24 g) za'atar (page 168)

½ tablespoon sumac (see page 148), plus a little extra for sprinkling

1 cup (250 g) low-fat Turkish or Greek yogurt (see page 126), divided

3 tablespoons mild olive oil

1 package triangular yufka dough (available at Middle Eastern grocery stores or online, see page 202)

2 cloves garlic

3 tablespoons butter

2 tablespoons Aleppo pepper (see page 44)

1 cup (100 g) pine nuts

- Preheat the oven to 400°F (205°C). Mince the red onion and mix it with the ground lamb, za'atar, and sumac; season with salt. Add the olive oil to 6 tablespoons (110 g) of the yogurt and stir lightly.
- Place the yufka sheets in front of you and cover with a clean kitchen towel to prevent them from drying out. Brush all sheets on both sides with the yogurt-oil. Arrange a very thin roll of ground lamb along the long edge of the dough and roll up the sheet. Repeat until you're out of dough. Place the rolls on a baking sheet lined with parchment paper and brush them with a little yogurt-oil. Bake for about 15 minutes, until golden brown and crispy, flipping them halfway through.
- Grate the garlic. In a small skillet, heat the butter with the Aleppo pepper, garlic, and pine nuts; fry until the nuts are golden brown. Season with salt. Stir some salt into the remaining yogurt. Serve the yufka rolls topped with the cold yogurt, then spoon the warm garlic–pine nut butter on top and sprinkle with a pinch of sumac.

Snobar

In Lebanese, pine nuts are called snobar, which sounds really cute. They may seem plain at first, but a nice pine cone contains about fifty pine nuts. So much work! Those Lebanese snobar are long and thick, very different from the more common, but inferior, small pine nuts. They are essential for an authentic, classic Lebanese hummus: mild and creamy from the chickpeas and tahini, and nutty from the pine nuts.

Keep cool

Keep nuts and nut oils in the fridge so they stay fresh. Nuts in general are essential in Middle Eastern cuisine: They give flavor, structure, and depth to salads, sauces, fillings, and all kinds of dishes. They are viewed as a key flavoring or even the main ingredient in many dishes.

Sem sem

"Sesame" stems from the Arbic *sem sem*, and that probably comes from the sound that the seed makes once it pops out of its skin. The Egyptians were kneading sesame seeds into their dough 4,000 years ago and they still do so today. In Syria and Lebanon, sesame seeds are mixed with za'atar. Sesame seed is, of course, the main ingredient of tahini, which we can't live without. No sesame seed, no life!

At the restaurant Koçak in Gaziantep, Turkey, we ate the most delicious baklava (they are famous for it!). The pistachio nuts are picked when they're still unripe, which gives them their characteristic taste and beautiful green color. *Baklava* means "diamond" in Turkish.

Young green almonds

If you've ever seen a blossoming almond tree, you know how romantic the almond can be. It's no wonder the almond is popularly turned into dragées (the Jordan almonds used as wedding favors) and even works as an aphrodisiac.

The nut contains a lot of mild almond oil. Almonds are also often soaked in water, which then is made into a delicious almond milk. Anyone who has used their teeth to crack open a young almond with a green, hairy skin knows how nice a young, milky almond tastes. We can't stop eating them. You can sometimes find them in Middles Eastern grocery stores in the spring.

Nut of the gods

Walnuts are called the nut of the gods—even the ancient Greeks used the oil from walnuts. In Iran they use ground walnuts to thicken the famous chicken stew called fesejan. Walnuts are also often used for baklava.

NUTS

Pistachios, sesame seeds, walnuts, almonds & pine nuts

A Bundt pan seemed to us a great way to bake a festive Arabic cake filled with poppy and sesame seeds. It's a rich cake and, when served with thick Turkish kaymakli yogurt and rose petal jam, a divine treat. You can find rose petal jam in Middle Eastern groceries, or you can make it yourself (see the recipe below) from handpicked, organic wild rose petals. You can also use another jam, such as fig jam, if you prefer.

Sesame and Poppy Seed Bundt Cake

With rose petal jam

SERVES 8 TO 10

1 scant cup (200 g) melted butter

1⅔ cups (200 g) all-purpose flour

1 cup (200 g) sugar

4 large eggs

⅓ cup (50 g) white sesame seeds

⅓ cup (50 g) poppy seeds

Rose petal jam (see recipe)

Kaymakli yogurt (see Note)

- Preheat the oven to 300°F (150°C). Generously grease an 8- to 10-inch (20- to 25-cm) Bundt pan with some butter and dust with flour.
- In a bowl, beat the butter, sugar, and a pinch of salt with a hand mixer for about 10 minutes, until light and creamy. Beat in the eggs one at a time, adding the next egg only after the previous one has been fully incorporated. Don't cheat—if you don't whisk for the full 10 minutes and add the eggs one at the time, you won't get a nice, airy cake!
- Sift the flour and fold it gently into the egg mixture, then fold in the sesame and poppy seeds. Pour the batter into the Bundt pan until it's three-quarters full. Smooth the surface with a knife or spatula.
- Bake for 1 to 1½ hours, until the cake is light brown and a skewer inserted in the center comes out clean and dry. Let cool in the pan, then invert the cake onto a rack and let cool further. Serve with a big scoop of rose petal jam and kaymakli yogurt.

NOTE: If you can't find kaymakli yogurt, you can mix 1¾ cups (400 g) full-fat Turkish or Greek yogurt with 1 cup (200 g) mascarpone cheese.

- ROSE PETAL JAM

  Heat 1 cup (200 g) plus 2 tablespoons gelling sugar (sugar with pectin) with ⅔ cup (165 ml) water, juice from half a lemon, and the petals of 10 organic, dark-red, fragrant roses. Stir well and let the jam thicken for about 15 minutes. Pour into a sterilized jar, let cool, and keep in the refrigerator.

Pistacchi di Bronte

SICILIAN PISTACHIOS

Pistachio nuts mostly hail from Turkey, Iran, Iraq, and Tunisia. The striking pistachio trees don't need much water and are able to grow in dry, desert-like areas. The Phoenicians and the Greeks introduced pistachios to Sicily, and the Sicilian pistachios from Bronte are famous for their flavor—we'll never forget the divine, deep-green pistachio ice cream that was made with those pistachios. Sicilian pistachio nuts, which are difficult to find, are not only longer and thinner than Middle Eastern pistachios, but also have a stronger flavor.

Cookies exist in countless variations and they often consist of the same base ingredients. These cookies are made from pine nuts and honey. You can make them at the spur of the moment, and serve them on a large platter and not in a closed box! Everyone loves these cookies—they're delicious with white coffee (hot water with a dash of orange blossom water) or Moroccan mint tea.

Hazelnut Honey Cookies
With pine nuts

SERVES 4 TO 6

1¼ cups (150 g) all-purpose flour

1 teaspoon baking powder

⅓ cup (75 g) sugar

⅔ cup (150 g) cold butter, in chunks

½ cup (50 g) hazelnuts, ground

10 tablespoons (150 ml) honey

2 tablespoons pine nuts

- Sift the flour with the baking powder and a pinch of salt into a mixing bowl, and then sift in the sugar. Cut the butter into the flour using two forks. Add the hazelnuts and honey and knead quickly into a smooth dough. Let the dough rest for at least 30 minutes in the fridge.
- Preheat the oven to 350°F (175°C). Line a baking sheet with parchment paper. On a flour-dusted countertop, roll out the dough into a 1½-inch-(4-cm-) thick rectangle. Cut out cookies with a glass rim or round cookie cutter. Decorate the cookies with pine nuts and place them all on the baking sheet. Form another dough ball from the scraps and repeat the process.
- Bake the cookies for about 10 minutes, until golden brown. Peel them carefully from the parchment while they're still warm. Let them cool and become crispy on a plate.

Fesenjan or *khoresht fesenjan* is the pride of Persian cuisine and garners applause in the entire Arab world. It is a combination of sweet-acidic fruit, with nuts and meat or poultry stew, which you'll find from Mecca to Marrakech. It's a very festive dish, traditionally made with duck, but we have used quail. We also have sprinkled the fesenjan with *advieh*: a heady Persian mixture of spices consisting of rose petals, cardamom, cinnamon, and cumin. Advieh is also a terrific seasoning for rice. For a truly sumptuous preparation, we add saffron to the advieh. If your butcher does not carry quail, it may be available as a special order; frozen quail can be ordered online.

Fesenjan with Quail

With pomegranate and walnuts

SERVES 4 TO 6

2 sweet onions

2 tablespoons butter

4 to 6 quails

1 pinch saffron

2½ cups (250 g) walnuts

2¾ cups (660 ml) pomegranate juice

2 tablespoons cinnamon

Rose water (see page 92)

5 tablespoons pine nuts

FOR THE ADVIEH

2 tablespoons cinnamon

2 tablespoons ground cardamom

2 tablespoons cumin

3 tablespoons dried edible rose petals (available at baking supply shops and online)

- Slice the onions in half-moons. Heat the butter in a Dutch oven and sauté the onions for 10 minutes over low heat. Add the quails and the saffron and fry the quails for 10 minutes on medium heat, until golden brown. Take the quails from the pan and cover to keep warm.
- Grind the walnuts and add them to the onions, along with the pomegranate juice and cinnamon. Season with salt and add some rose water to taste. Let the sauce simmer for 30 minutes on very low heat. Add the quails and simmer for another 15 minutes on low heat. If the sauce becomes too thick, add a dash of water.

- FOR THE ADVIEH

Mix the cinnamon with the cardamom, cumin, and rose petals. Sprinkle over the finished dish and serve the remaining advieh separately.

Kataifi dough dates back to the Ottoman Empire; the finely shredded phyllo dough is spun as thin and beautiful as angel hair! Across Syria and the eastern Mediterranean, it is used in sweet dishes like this kanafeh (a Levantine cheese pastry). We made this quick kanafeh from kaymakli (thick Turkish yogurt), with anise, pistachio nuts, and figs. To make it really Arabic, we pour some sugar syrup over it before serving. You'll find kataifi dough in vacuum-sealed packages in the bread section of Middle Eastern grocery stores.

Kanafeh

With pistachio-anise kaymakli and figs

SERVES 6 TO 8

⅔ cup (165 ml) milk

½ cup (115 g) butter

10½ ounces (300 g) kataifi

1 cup (200 g) sugar

3 cups (600 g) kaymakli yogurt (see Note)

10 soft dried figs

1 cup (100 g) pistachio nuts

1 teaspoon anise seed

- Preheat the oven to 400°F (205°C). Heat the milk with the butter and set aside to cool. Pull the kataifi apart in a large bowl and pour the cooled butter mixture over it. Mix well and set aside to steep.
- Butter a shallow round cake pan or baking dish, and press the kataifi firmly in an even layer to cover the bottom of the pan. Bake for about 40 minutes, until golden brown and crispy. Meanwhile, in a small pot, combine ¾ cup (180 ml) water with the sugar. Bring to a boil and reduce to a thick syrup. Let cool.
- Put the kaymakli in a bowl; pull the figs open and arrange them over the kaymakli. Sprinkle with the pistachio nuts and anise seed. Serve with kataifi and the cooled syrup.

NOTE: Can't find kaymakli? Mix 1¾ cups (400 g) full-fat Turkish or Greek yogurt with 1 cup (200 g) mascarpone cheese.

We've seen several sorts of nuts, such as ras el hanout nuts, across the Middle East. The combination of spices and nuts—sweet and salty—remains irresistible. Like the Arabs, we're fanatic nut eaters.

Sweet-Salty Nuts

With citrus and fennel seed

SERVES 4 TO 8

Grated zest of 1 orange, divided

Grated zest of 1 lemon, divided

2 tablespoons fennel seed

3 cups (300 g) mixed salted nuts

¾ cup (150 g) sugar

- With a mortar and pestle, pound half of the citrus zest with the fennel seed.
- Heat the nuts with the sugar in a skillet over low heat, stirring constantly. Keep stirring until there's a thin coating of melted sugar on the nuts, then add the citrus-fennel mixture along with the rest of the citrus zest. Spoon the nuts onto a baking sheet lined with parchment paper and let cool. Toss occasionally so they don't stick together.
- Before serving, sprinkle the nuts with some extra sea salt. Store in an airtight container.

Whenever there's a celebration, you eat rice!

In the Middle East, there are two methods of preparing rice: the Turkish way and the Iranian way. The Iranian way is the most elaborate. The rice is thoroughly washed in water—every grain is rubbed loose between the fingers, while the water is replaced several times. Afterward, the rice is soaked in salted water for several hours, and then it is strained and cooked in ample salted water. It cooks for only a few minutes, and when the rice is ready the grains are strained right away. To finish the cooking, the rice is simmered for another half hour in a pan with butter and a little water or bouillon, and covered with a clean kitchen towel. (The towel absorbs the excess steam, making sure the rice doesn't stay too moist.) This white rice is called challow. When you add flavors by mixing in vegetables and meat, it becomes pallow. This method is complicated, but the result is amazing. We've been able to experience this many times when visiting Gala, our "Afghani mother-in-law," who prepares large quantities of rice this way. Then there are the Turks. They keep things a lot simpler: The rice is washed only once, then it's cooked in a measured amount of water or bouillon with butter, oil, and/or spices. Sometimes the raw rice is first fried in oil or butter, and then meat, vegetables, water, and/or bouillon are added (this is similar to the risotto method, or pilaf, which is a variation on pallow).

Here's our advice: On weekdays use the Turkish method and on the weekends, or when there's a party, do as the Iranians do!

What do the people of paradise eat? "Rice in butter."

Which rice?

The best-quality rice is basmati. With its beautiful long, white grains, this rice isn't cheap, but it's excellent for Iranian and Middle Eastern rice dishes. Turkish rice, for making pilaf, is short-grain rice, similar to the Italian rice used to make risotto. Both types can be found in abundance in Middle Eastern grocery store.

The irresistible golden crust

The golden crust that forms on the bottom of the pan when cooking rice is a delicacy over which people often quarrel. Who gets to eat it? Naturally, it's the cook's privilege! A good trick for loosening the crust is to submerge the pan in cold water for a few minutes.

Izz bi'l rizz wu'l burghul yeshni nafsu

"Good living is with the rice and let the bulgur hang itself."

—A Syrian proverb

—Source: Sarat Zubaida, *Rice in the Culinary Cultures of the Middle East*

RICE

Most likely the origin of maqlooba, or maqloobeh, lies in historic Palestine, but you can find this dish everywhere in the Levant (Lebanon, Israel, Syria, and Jordan). Maqlooba is made with eggplant, cauliflower, and sometimes even chestnuts. It's often combined with lamb stew, but for this version we've purposely just used eggplant. Don't be fooled by these simple ingredients; maqlooba is heavenly and a true festival dish! Our version is a layered maqlooba. Less elegant perhaps than the eggplant-pie version (for which you place all eggplant at the bottom of the pan and then flip it over after cooking), but this is how we like it best. Yogurt is the classic condiment. We stir in some dill for an extra punch of flavor.

Maqlooba

With eggplant and fresh dill yogurt

SERVES 4

2 large onions

2 tablespoons clarified butter

1 to 3 tablespoons 7-spices (page 172)

4 eggplants

Mild olive oil

1½ cups (300 g) rice

1 cinnamon stick

¾ cup (75 g) almonds

1 bunch dill

1½ cups (300 g) Turkish or Greek yogurt (see page 126)

• Cut the onions into half-moon slices. Heat the butter in a skillet and sauté the onions with the 7-spices and a pinch of salt for 15 minutes over low heat. Meanwhile, thinly slice the eggplants lengthwise and, in a deep skillet, deep-fry them in a generous layer of oil until golden brown. Drain on paper towels and sprinkle with salt.

• Remove the onion mixture from the pan. Rinse the rice and drain. Coat a deep skillet with olive oil. Layer some eggplant slices in the skillet, ladle the onions and half of the rice on top, and season with salt. Cover with another eggplant layer, another layer of rice, and a pinch of salt, then finish with the rest of the eggplant. Add 2½ cups (600 ml) water, the cinnamon stick, and a pinch of salt, cover, and bring to a simmer. Lower the heat to very low and cook the maqlooba for 15 minutes. Remove from the heat and let the maqlooba rest for another 5 minutes.

• In a small skillet, deep-fry the almonds in oil over medium heat until golden brown, about 5 minutes. Let cool and finely chop them. Mince the dill and stir it into the yogurt along with some salt.

• Remove the cinnamon stick from the pan. Spoon or invert the maqlooba onto a serving dish, sprinkle with the almonds, and serve yogurt on the side.

In Egypt kushari (or koshari), a mixture of lentils and rice topped with pasta, is eaten as street food. There are special kushari carts and restaurants that serve all the ingredients piled on top of one another in a little bowl—like a kushari buffet. You eat it with spicy chili sauce and lemon wedges. You've only truly visited Egypt once you've eaten kushari. We make a kushari mix, with vermicelli, rice, lentils, and chickpeas all stirred together instead of separated in layers. It's traditionally a poor man's dish, but when it is served in a nice large bowl, the riches of its flavors are abundant.

Kushari

SERVES 4 TO 8

6 large onions

Mild olive oil

½ cup (100 g) chickpeas (soaked overnight, see page 82)

2 (14-ounce/400-g) cans peeled tomatoes

3½ ounces (100 g) vermicelli

¾ cup (150 g) rice

½ cup (100 g) lentils (Le Puy or brown lentils, see page 82)

1 tablespoon butter

2 cloves garlic

2 tablespoons ground cumin

1 tablespoon Aleppo pepper (see page 44)

Juice of 1 lemon

Dukkah (page 164)

- Cut the onions into half-moon slices. Heat a generous splash of oil in a skillet and brown two-thirds of the onions for 15 minutes, turning them continuously. Add a pinch of salt. Drain the onions on a paper towel. Meanwhile, cook the chickpeas in ample water for about 45 minutes, until tender. Heat a splash of oil in a skillet and sauté the rest of the onions on low heat for about 10 minutes, until translucent. Add the tomatoes and a little salt and reduce to a thick sauce over low heat, about 30 minutes. Toast the vermicelli in a dry skillet for about 3 minutes, until it's light brown all over. Allow to cool.

- Put the rice and the lentils in a heavy-bottomed pan. Add enough water to cover the rice and lentils by about ½ inch (12 mm). Add the butter and some salt. Bring to a boil, stir thoroughly, cover with a lid, and boil for about 20 minutes on low heat, until al dente. Add the vermicelli to the rice and lentils for the last 5 minutes of cooking time; if they have become too dry, add some boiling water. Remove the pan from the heat, but don't uncover the pot; let steam for a while, then stir.

- Crush the garlic and some coarse salt with a mortar and pestle, add the ground cumin, Aleppo pepper, and lemon juice and grind thoroughly. Put this mixture in a bowl and stir in 6 tablespoons of the tomato sauce. Drain the chickpeas and combine them with the rice mixture. Serve the kushari with the tomato sauce and the garlic-tomato pasta; spoon the fried onions on top. Sprinkle the kushari generously with dukkah just before serving.

Gala Parwien Sana is married into our family. She's originally from Afghanistan and she's a marvelous cook. Her rice is legendary. If she makes rice and Merijn is not there, Nadia simply *has* to bring her a portion. This rice is sweet, spicy, and seductive. It tastes great with or without meat. In countries like Pakistan, Iran, India, and Afghanistan, it's all about the rice—the quality of a cook's rice is the ultimate proof of his or her mastery of the kitchen.

Gala's Golden Rice

With orange and lamb stew

SERVES 4 TO 6

2½ pounds (1 kg) boneless lamb shoulder, for stewing

2 small onions

Peanut oil

2 tablespoons advieh (see page 222)

1 large carrot

1⅓ cups (200 g) large yellow raisins (available at Middle Eastern groceries)

2 tablespoons dried chopped orange peel, or 1 tablespoon ground (available at Middle Eastern grocery stores; see Note)

2¾ cups (500 g) basmati rice (washed and drained, see page 228)

⅓ cup (75 g) butter

- Chop the meat into bite-size pieces and mince the onions. Heat a good amount of olive oil in a Dutch oven and brown the meat all over, working in batches if necessary to avoid crowding the pot. Add the onions, the advieh, and some salt and cook for 10 minutes over low heat. Add enough water to almost cover the meat. Cover with a lid and stew for 1½ to 2 hours over low heat, until very tender.
- Peel and grate the carrot. Steep the raisins and the orange peels in water to cover until they're nicely swollen from absorbed water. Drain well.
- In a large pan, bring ample water to a boil and add some salt. Add the rice and simmer for about 5 minutes, until al dente, and thoroughly drain in a large strainer. Combine the rice with the carrot, raisins, orange peel, and butter in the strainer. Then ladle everything back into the pan (don't scoop it all in at once, or the rice will not be fluffy). Using the handle end of a wooden spoon, punch a few steam holes all the way through untill you hit the bottom. Wrap the lid of your rice pan in a clean kitchen towel. Put the lid on the pot and allow the rice to gently steam for another 20 minutes over very low heat. Leave the rice covered until you're ready to serve it. Serve Gala's rice with the lamb stew.

NOTE: If you can't find dried orange peels, thinly slice the zest of 2 oranges. Briefly cook the strips in boiling water, then rinse them immediately with cold water. The peels will taste a little bitter. If the bitterness is not to your taste, repeat the cooking process twice more with clean water. You can add the blanched peels directly to the rice with the soaked raisins.

We love salads with tasty grains and lots of flavor! The 7-spices dressing instantly gives this salad Lebanese character, and it tastes heavenly with the nuts and raisins. This is also great with a handful of sea beans mixed in. Delicious as a lunch salad, but also great with fried or roasted fish or with kebab.

Herbed Rice Salad

With pistachios, almonds, and 7-spices dressing

SERVES 2 TO 4

¾ cup (135 g) basmati rice

¾ cup (135 g) red rice

⅔ cup (100 g) currants

1 white onion

2 tablespoons red wine vinegar

6 tablespoons (90 ml) fruity green olive oil

2 teaspoons 7-spices (page 172)

1 cup (100 g) roasted almonds

1 cup (100 g) roasted pistachio nuts

1 bunch cilantro

1 bunch flat-leaf parsley

- In separate pots, cook the basmati and red rices in ample salted water until al dente. Meanwhile, soak the currants in water. Drain the rice and cool it by rinsing with cold water. Allow to drain.
- Coarsely chop the onion, place it in a large measuring cup, and add the vinegar, oil, and 7-spices. Process into a creamy dressing with a hand blender. Add salt and some extra vinegar or 7-spices if needed, to taste.
- Coarsely chop the almonds and pistachios. Do the same with the cilantro and parsley. Drain the currants. Just before serving, mix the cooked rice, currants, nuts, cilantro, and parsley in a large bowl and dress to taste.

Golden argan oil

A few years ago we were in a tiny village just outside of Essaouira, Morocco. It is a town in the middle of nowhere, where local women taught us how to crack argan nuts and how to squeeze out the oil with our bare hands. We were sitting on the ground using a rock to crack open the nuts of the remarkable argan tree. The trick was to open up the nut with one firm, well-placed knock without damaging the argan pit, which resembles a pumpkin seed. It didn't take long before we had the trick down and were carefully opening the nuts one by one, earning admiring looks: We belonged. Afterward, the pits were roasted and ground with a special stone pestle. The resulting thick paste was kneaded with water, separating a golden-brown oil of unparalleled flavor. That's when we understood why this oil is so expensive. Argan trees grow only in the Souss Valley, in the triangle between the towns of Essaouira, Agadir, and Safi. Goats love them. They climb the trees to eat the nuts. It's said that the nuts are even better after they've been eaten, fermented, and discharged from the bowels of these goats!

Argan oil comes in many different qualities. The color has to be a beautiful golden brown and the smell wonderfully nutty. In some Middle Eastern groceries you'll see empty soda bottles filled with argan oil. Sometimes these self-imported oils are superb; sometimes they are terrible! Always inspect the oil closely and smell it before you buy. But remember: Argan oil should never be cheap. Argan oil is also very popular in the cosmetic world as a hair and skin treatment, so make sure that what you're buying is meant to be used in the kitchen!

It's delicious as a flavoring in soups, couscous, or tajines and, mixed with ground almonds and honey, it's also wonderful as a dip (when it's called amlou). Eat it for breakfast with fresh baked bread. We prefer to buy our argan oil from certified women's cooperatives, so that the local Moroccan women get a fair price for their goods. Argan oil is best stored in the fridge. That way it will keep for a long time.

Kneaded butter

Smen, or samneh or smin, is a flavorful cooking ingredient from Moroccan cuisine. It's really just rancid or fermented farm butter. But this is not just any butter—the taste is complex and savory, almost like a ripened French cheese or aged Parmesan. There are several ways to make smen (see the recipe on page 248). The salty smen is perfect for flavoring couscous, but also for seasoning sauces and soups. But take care: If you're unfamiliar with the taste, start by using just a dash!

SMEN & ARGAN OIL

Sometimes root vegetables, which are naturally delicious, need nothing more than enough time to cook slowly and a sprinkling of fermented, spicy smen and crunchy almonds.

Root Vegetable Tajine

With smen and almonds

SERVES 4

2 sweet onions

Mild olive oil

2 sweet potatoes

1 small butternut squash

1 small carrot

4 turnips

4 Jerusalem artichokes

4 small beets

⅓ cup (75 g) smen (page 248), divided

¾ cup (75 g) almonds

• Cut the onions into half-moon slices. Heat some oil in a tajine or Dutch oven and sauté the onions for 10 minutes over low heat. Clean and peel the potatoes, squash, carrot, turnips, Jerusalem artichokes, and beets and chop them in chunks. Add the vegetables to the tajine with some salt, 1 tablespoon of the smen, and ¾ cup (180 ml) water. Slowly cook the tajine for 45 minutes over low heat. You can occasionally add some water if the tajine becomes too dry.

• In a skillet, fry the almonds in a good amount of oil until golden brown and crunchy. Drain, allow to cool, and then chop fine. Sprinkle small flakes of the remaining smen and the almonds over the tajine. Serve immediately.

While attending the celebration of a newborn somewhere near Casablanca, Morocco, we were so fascinated by the description of this golden-yellow semolina soup with saffron and garlic from Rabia Dahhan that we had trouble focusing on the roasted lamb with cumin placed on the table in front of us.

Light Semolina Soup

With garlic-saffron bouillon and argan oil

SERVES 4

2 tablespoons butter

3 gloves garlic

Pinch of saffron threads

1½ cups (250 g) fine semolina

Argan oil (see page 238)

- Heat the butter in a skillet and sauté the garlic for 10 minutes over low heat. Add the saffron and then stir in the semolina. Add 2 cups (480 ml) water and bring to a boil while stirring constantly. Season with salt.
- Gently cook the semolina soup for about 25 minutes over low heat. You can add some water if needed—the soup shouldn't become too thick, but remain creamy and light. Before serving, drizzle the soup with the argan oil.

A DOWRY!
In some Berber communities in southern Morocco, smen is used as dowry. When a daughter is born, the family buries a ceramic jar with fresh smen in the ground. On the day of her wedding, the jar is unearthed and the smen is used for the festive dinner. You can imagine how strong and intense the taste has become!

In Essaouira, Morocco, there's always a soft, salty sea breeze, and it's a real treat to eat a breakfast of freshly baked bread with amlou: ground almonds with argan oil and honey. In this version we also add some hazelnuts and anise seed.

Sometimes you can find amlou ready-made in Middle Eastern grocery stores, sold in plastic jars with blue lids. The argan oil sold in these stores is usually of good quality as well, but just remember: There's no such thing as cheap argan oil.

Amlou

From almonds and hazelnuts with anise

SERVES 4

1 cup (100 g) blanched almonds

1 cup (100 g) blanched hazelnuts

¾ cup (180 ml) argan oil (see page 238)

1 tablespoon anise seed

Honey

• In a food processor, grind the almonds, hazelnuts, argan oil, and anise seed; add honey to taste. Serve the amlou with freshly baked bread. It's also great with strong Arabian coffee.

It's really fun to make your own delicious smen. If you live in an area where raw-milk products are available, it's worth the effort to seek out a local dairy that sells raw-milk butter. Otherwise, choose very fresh unsalted butter of the best quality. Smen is great for seasoning steamed couscous; you can mix it with harira or use it to finish tajines. It tastes wonderful on toast with fresh figs, served with a cup of Moraccan mint tea.

Herbed Smen

SERVES 10

2¼ cups (605 g) raw-milk butter or fresh, best-quality unsalted butter

2 sprigs rosemary

2 sprigs oregano

2 sprigs thyme

- With your hands, knead the butter with the rosemary, oregano, thyme, a little water, and 1 tablespoon coarse sea salt. Then put the butter in a sterilized jar and store in a cool, dark place. Let it ferment for a couple of weeks, but remove the herb sprigs from the butter after about a week.

- Here's an alternative method: Clarify the butter by heating it with the herbs and/or a cinnamon stick for 30 minutes over low heat. Pour the melted butter through a fine-mesh sieve so that the white milk curds and the herbs stay behind. Pour the clarified butter into a clean jar (scalded or cleaned in the dishwasher), add 1 tablespoon sea salt, seal, then store for several weeks in a cool, dark place.

Markook

Markook is the typical flatbread of the Levant. You'll find it everywhere in Lebanon. Look for it here in Middle Eastern grocery stores or bakeries; it can also be ordered online. *Markook* means "thin" in Arabic and the bread can be stretched as large and thin as a tablecloth. It's made from large sheets of dough. This is done by women who sit on the ground with large, round, floured pillows on their laps, on which they manage to convert little balls of risen dough in a pizza-like fashion into thin, almost translucent sheets. The stretched dough is baked on a *saj*, a large convex metal griddle. The pillow is used to "throw" the sheet of dough onto the hot pan. The bread is ready in a few seconds. We've tried to replicate the cooking process on an upside-down wok. The result wasn't quite like a real markook, but it produced a lovely thin flatbread nonetheless.

Khobz Arabi (Arabic flatbread)

In Lebanon and Syria nearly everything is eaten with flatbread, and by that we mean a really flat bread: a kind of round, flat cushion from which you keep tearing little pieces that you use to pick up bites of food. Because the bread dries out very quickly, it's served on the table in plastic bags. In Lebanon and Syria they do this even in restaurants. Once in the Bab Touma section of Damascus, Syria, we spotted open bags of freshly baked flatbreads steaming on the hood of a car. On the island of Sardinia, they make an almost identical type of bread, but there they cut it in half and bake it a second time, turning it into crispy, paper-thin *pane carasau* (or Italian flatbread).

Moroccan bread

This type of yeast-leavened bread is usually made from a combination of wheat flour and semolina and baked in the oven. It comes in white and whole-wheat versions, small and large, and it's always eaten with dinner. Once again bread is used as a utensil. It's the custom to eat only with your right hand, using two or at most three fingers. This bread is indispensable when eating tajine. The crumb perfectly absorbs all the delicious sauce left at the end (see page 256).

Rghaif

Also called msemen. This breakfast staple starts with unleavened bread dough made from wheat flour and semolina. It has a pastry-like structure and looks a bit like a cross between bread, phyllo dough, and a pancake—it's sublime when served warm with honey and/or olive oil. The mark of a good host is one who gets up early in the morning to bake some fresh rghaif for guests.

Pita

The world-famous pita can be found in Israel, Egypt, Greece, the Balkans, and the rest of the Middle East. Some versions are a mix between khobz Arabi and pita. The pita bread found in most supermarkets has little to do with the real thing. Pita bread should be soft and freshly baked.

Simit and Ka'ak

Simit is a moderately sweet white bread ring that is baked in an oven and comes with or without sesame seeds. Ka'ak is a kind of oval-shaped envelope of sweet dough that comes with a variety of sweet or savory fillings—or often za'atar. In Egypt, ka'ak is eaten with dukkah. In Beirut ka'ak is street food, and the sellers are still an integral part of the streetscape with their ka'ak bikes or mopeds.

Where to buy

It is always best to buy bread freshly baked, so look for Turkish, Lebanese, and Moroccan bakeries in larger cities; Middle Eastern grocery stores will have a selection of different flatbreads, and you can also purchase many types online. For truly fresh bread, however, you'll have to start baking yourself.

Harsha

A Moroccan bread made from semolina and butter and pan-fried; these small, round cakes resemble crumpets. For breakfast or as a snack, you can eat it with honey or amlou, a Moroccan dip made from toasted almonds, argan oil, and honey. (page 246)

In the Arab world, bread is sacred. In the words of the Palestinian poet Mahmoud Darwish, bread is a metaphor for motherly love, home, and peace. "I long for my mother's bread . . ." begins his poem "My Mother." Bread is eaten with every meal; it is almost always a flatbread, and is often used as an eating utensil in and of itself.

BREAD

Turkish pide

We've never actually seen the Turkish pide (that country's version of flatbread) in Turkey. We did, however, spot the characteristic thinner Turkish bread, which is soft and a bit elastic, has white crumb, and is baked with sesame seeds. The dough has a relatively high water content.

Fkakes, also called fkajes, are traditional cookies of northern Morocco. *Fkakes* roughly translates to "frustrating," and as it happens this dough does take a lot of kneading, attention, and time. But the result is something unique. We got this recipe from Galtoe Assia, who's famous for her superb fkakes throughout the Dutch town of Winterswijk. Being twice-baked, these pastries are the Moroccan answer to Italian biscotti—perfect for dunking in tea, coffee, vin santo, or Moroccan fig brandy.

Fkakes

MAKES ABOUT 16 SOFT BUNS OR 112 CRISP SLICES

1 tablespoon smen (page 248)

½ cup (115 g) butter

1 scant tablespoon gum mastic pieces, or about 3 teaspoons ground meska horra (available at Middle Eastern groceries or online)

8 cups (1 kg) all-purpose flour

½ tablespoon sesame seeds

½ tablespoon anise seed

1¼ cups (250 g) sugar, plus an extra ½ teaspoon

6½ tablespoons (92 ml) orange blossom water (see page 92)

1 tablespoon fresh yeast, or 1 teaspoon instant yeast

- Melt the smen with the butter. Crush the mastic with a mortar and pestle. Combine the flour, mastic, sesame seeds, and anise seed in the bowl of an electric stand mixer. Form a small well in the center of the flour mixture and spoon in the 1¼ cups (250 g) sugar. Pour the hot butter onto the sugar and gently stir so the sugar will begin to melt. Bit by bit fold the butter into the sugar-flour mixture, then beat with the mixer's dough hook to form a dough. Add the orange blossom water bit by bit and continue beating for at least 5 minutes.
- Meanwhile, in a separate bowl, stir the yeast with the ½ teaspoon sugar, ¼ cup (60 ml) warm water, and a tiny piece of the dough from the other bowl. Allow to rise for 15 minutes, while still beating the dough in the mixer.
- Add the yeast mix to the dough in the bowl and beat for another 30 minutes (this dough needs a lot of kneading!),

adding some lukewarm water to help it come together (up to about ¾ cup/180 ml), but don't let the dough become too sticky; it should be rather firm and still supple. Form the dough into a loaf and cut it into thick slices, then pat every slice into a small, flat roll. Keep the dough covered with clean kitchen towels or a folded tablecloth. Let rise in a draft-free, warm place for 2 to 4 hours; the rolls will remain fairly flat.

- Preheat the oven to 300°F (150°C). Stamp a nice shape deeply into the top of each roll (we've carved a pomegranate into a half potato). Pierce every roll once with a needle. Bake the fkakes for about 30 minutes. The crust should still be white to light brown. If they begin to brown too fast, lower the oven temperature.
- By now the fkakes are already delicious, but if you like crunchy bread, slice them and bake them again in a 400°F (205°C) oven until golden brown. This also happens to be a great way to revive stale fkakes!

We no longer know what to call these delicious bread-pancakes. Some say rghaif and others call them msemen. Whatever you call them, they're great, and we simply love to make them for a luxurious breakfast surprise.

Rghaif

MAKES 6 PIECES

1½ cups (200 g) all-purpose flour

1¼ cups (200 g) fine semolina, plus 2 to 3 tablespoons for dusting

1 tablespoon fresh yeast, or 1 teaspoon instant yeast

½ teaspoon sugar

6 tablespoons (90 ml) sunflower oil

6 tablespoons (85 g) butter, melted

- Combine the flour and the semolina in a large, shallow bowl. Form a well in the center, pour in the yeast, and add the sugar. Pour a little lukewarm water over the yeast, dissolving it a bit. Sprinkle the flour around the edges of the bowl with about 1 teaspoon salt, but make sure the salt doesn't come in contact with the yeast (this will disrupt the fermentation). Then gradually mix the flour with the yeast mixture and, while kneading, add about 1 cup (240 ml) lukewarm water. Knead into a soft, smooth dough. If the dough is hard to knead, let it rest on the counter for 5 minutes before continuing to knead.
- Divide the dough into 12 small balls. In a bowl, mix the oil with the butter. Use this to thoroughly grease your hands. Grease a piece of parchment paper, place the balls on top, and drizzle with a little of the oil-butter mixture. Flatten a ball with your hands and spread it into as thin a rectangle as possible. Don't worry if you make some holes in it. Lightly sprinkle the flattened dough with some semolina, drizzle with a little of the oil-butter mixture, and fold it loosely into thirds as if folding a letter. Set aside. Flatten another ball and spread it into a thin rectangle. Then place the folded piece of dough on top of the flattened sheet. Again lightly sprinkle with semolina and drizzle with the oil-butter mixture. Fold into a flat package and gently press together. Heat a dry nonstick skillet (or a special rghaif pan, sold in some Middle Eastern stores) and cook the rghaif until golden brown and crisp on both sides, 8 to 10 minutes total.
- Repeat this process to create 6 packages in total. You can also fold all of them at once and then place them in a preheated 400°F (205°C) oven and bake until golden brown, 25 to 30 minutes, turning them over with a spatula halfway through. Served with some honey and salted butter, these are the perfect breakfast!

Back in the day, the neighborhood kids would all flock to Mama Dilla's (Nadia's mother) kitchen window when they smelled her freshly baked bread. Fadila used to bake two large loaves every day: one with melted butter and peanut butter, to give out to the children, and one for herself, to serve with that day's tajine. There still are few things that beat the smell of freshly baked bread. And we still honor the tradition of baking and giving out bread with love.

Mama Fadila's Bread

MAKES 2 LOAVES

4 cups (500 g) all-purpose flour, plus a little extra for dusting

3 cups (500 g) fine semolina

2 tablespoons fresh yeast, or 2 teaspoons instant yeast

¼ cup (60 ml) sunflower oil

1 large egg, beaten

4 tablespoons (36 g) white sesame seeds

- Combine the flour and the semolina in a large, shallow bowl. Form a well in the center, pour in the yeast, and add the sugar. Pour lukewarm water over the yeast, dissolving it a bit. Sprinkle the flour around the edges with about ½ teaspoon salt, but make sure the salt doesn't come in contact with the yeast (this will disrupt the fermentation).

- Gradually mix the flour with the yeast mixture and, while kneading, add about 2 cups (480 ml) lukewarm water. Knead for about 20 minutes to form a soft, smooth dough. Divide the dough in half. Cover with clean kitchen towels or a folded tablecloth. Let rise in a draft-free, warm place until they've doubled in size; this should take about 1½ hours. Place one half of the dough in front of you on a flour-dusted work surface and, with floured hands, flatten the dough into a round about 1¼ inch (3 cm) thick. Repeat with the other half. Cover again and let rest in a warm place to slightly rise for about 30 minutes.

- Preheat the oven to 400°F (205°C). Use your finger to punch a steam hole in the middle of each loaf—like a little navel—and pierce several times with a fork. Lightly glaze with some beaten egg and sprinkle with sesame seeds. Bake the loaves one by one for about 25 minutes, until golden brown.

- This is the ideal bread for absorbing—and devouring—all sorts of delicious tajine sauces.

In Morocco, during the month of Ramadan, you'll see towering stashes of *chebakkia*, dripping with honey, everywhere you look. They are a kind of crunchy, deep-fried, golden-brown nest, made from orange blossom dough with sesame seeds. Making the nests is time consuming and complicated (as well as fun). Here we opt for an easier way and cut the dough into beautiful cookies, which we then deep-fry. Chebakkia are traditionally eaten with harira (page 14).

Chebakkia

SERVES 6 TO 8

½ cup (75 g) toasted sesame seeds, plus a few extra for sprinkling

¾ cup (75 g) hazelnuts

3 cups (400 g) all-purpose flour

1 egg yolk

5 tablespoons (75 ml) orange blossom water (see page 92), plus a little extra to go with the honey

5 tablespoons (75 ml) sunflower oil

1½ tablespoons melted butter

1 teaspoon vinegar

½ teaspoon active dry or instant yeast

½ teaspoon ground anise seed

Frying oil

1¼ cups (300 ml) honey

- Finely grind the sesame seeds and the hazelnuts. In a bowl, combine the nuts with the flour, egg yolk, orange blossom water, sunflower oil, butter, vinegar, yeast, and anise seed. Add enough lukewarm water to form a dough (about ¾ cup/180 ml). Knead the dough by hand, or use an electric stand mixer fitted with a dough hook, until the dough is no longer sticky and has become nicely soft and supple. Roll the dough out thinly on a flour-dusted counter and cut or punch out some interesting shapes. Here we cut squares in which we carved a nice pattern.

- Heat an ample layer of oil in a wok or an electric frying pan set to 350°F (175°C). If using a wok, test whether the oil is hot enough by dropping in a piece of bread. It should immediately come floating to the surface looking golden brown. Meanwhile, in a saucepan over low heat, slowly heat the honey with a bit of orange blossom water to taste. Leave this on the heat while you fry the chebakkia; it should stay liquid but not boil.

- Fry a few chebakkia at a time until golden brown. Use a skimmer to spoon them out of the hot oil and immediately transfer them to the pan of honey. Turn them in the honey and transfer them to a strainer placed over a bowl (to collect the honey). In the strainer, sprinkle the chebakkia with a dash of sesame seeds. Continue frying the chebakkia until you're out of dough. If the strainer gets too full, transfer some pastries to a plate. If properly sealed in a plastic bag, chebakkia keep for a long time. They're tasty with harira (page 14), but also with a glass of Moroccan mint tea.

Inspired by markook, the gorgeous paper-thin, tablecloth-size bread grilled on the saj, and the nicely bulging pita, we made simple bread dough, which we bake on an upside-down wok or in the oven. That way, we have our very own Arabic flatbread. If you coat your flatbread with a mixture of za'atar and olive oil, you have man'ouche, the famous Lebanese bread that you can roll up into a cucumber, tomato, and cheese or labneh wrap and eat for breakfast. These are ideal breads for your mezze table. Use them as utensils for eating hummus and labneh.

Our Own Arabian Flatbread

SERVES 4

1 tablespoon fresh yeast, or 1 teaspoon instant yeast

½ tablespoon sugar

4 cups (500 g) all-purpose flour, plus extra for dusting

- Dissolve the yeast with the sugar in 6½ tablespoons (92 ml) lukewarm water. Combine the flour and 1 tablespoon salt in a large, shallow bowl. Form a well in the center and pour in the yeast mixture. Gradually combine the flour with the yeast mixture and, while kneading, add about ¾ cup (180 ml) lukewarm water. On a flour-dusted countertop, keep kneading until the dough no longerfeels sticky, but has become smooth and elastic. Cover with a clean kitchen towel or a folded tablecloth and set in a draft-free, warm place for about 30 minutes. Then divide the dough into eight small balls (for pitas) and five large ones (for flatbread).

- FOR PITA ROLLS: gently flatten the balls with your hands and let them rest for 10 minutes, covered with a clean kitchen towel, on a flour-dusted counter. Meanwhile, preheat the oven to the highest possible temperature, preferably 500°F (260°C), and place a pizza stone on the bottom. (If you don't have a pizza stone, thoroughly clean the oven bottom to use as your baking surface.)

- Roll out the balls as thin as you can—and by that we mean really thin! Place no more than 2 or 3 pitas simultaneously on the pizza stone and wait about 2 minutes, until they bulge and turn light brown. Remove the pitas from the oven, and immediately close the door so no heat escapes. Repeat for the rest of the rolls.

- FOR FLATBREAD: Place a wok, bottom up, on the burner and let it heat up. Thoroughly flatten one of the large dough balls and bake directly on the hot bottom of the wok. After mere seconds the bread will start to brown and to bulge. Bake for 1 to 2 minutes, until the underside is golden brown and starts to come loose from the wok bottom. Repeat with the remaining dough.

Ingmar Niezen

Ingmar, a wonderful food stylist, has been our highly esteemed colleague for many years. We learned a lot from her during our first forays into food styling. She was born and raised in South Africa and is the author of *The New African Cookbook*. Naturally, we often discuss Arabian influences in African cooking with her. The recipe for tamaaya, which we learned from her, is an obvious example.

Reem Albacha

Reem is our Syrian friend, who regularly fills up our fridges with ma'moul (shortbread cookies filled with walnuts and dates), falafel, and stuffed vegetables: dolmas and sarmas. A fantastic cook from Damascus, she's married to an Iraqi, and now lives in the Netherlands. For us she is an invaluable resource on the art of Middle Eastern cooking who looks to us for inspiration in return.

FRIENDS

Kamal Mouzawak

For anyone who knows us a little, Kamal no longer needs an introduction. He's the founder of Souk el Tayeb, the first organic farmer's market in Beirut, Lebanon. His idea of connecting people through food—"Make food, not war" —makes him a shining example to us all. He's become a beloved friend, who always welcomes us to his house and dinner table with an open heart, and we gladly return the invitation.

Mina Abouzahra

What can we tell you about our lovely Mina? Together with Mina, Merijn wrote her first cookbook *Orange Blossom* (which includes a recipe by Nadia). She is a dear friend. These days, besides being a fanatical cook, Mina is also a furniture designer. She makes beautiful pillows from antique Moroccan fabrics and Scandinavian Kvadrat felt. Her Gazella table and her pillows are featured on pages 274–75. Mina loves quinces.

Shahar Cohen

We came to know Shahar through our friend, who manages a farmer's market. Film- and hummus-maker Shahar hails from Jerusalem but now lives in Amsterdam and has become our enthusiastic cooking companion. Nothing is more delightful than going grocery shopping with him and returning to our kitchens to start cooking something mouthwatering like silky soft hummus, made with 100 percent love and attention, or his delightful Yemenite chicken soup. When everything is ready, we cover the table with food, and friends from all over gather to join us for dinner.

Shish barak is also known as *sourat bent al malik*: "the king's daughter's navel." Making this filled pasta takes quite some time, so this is a recipe for the true Middle Eastern epicureans among you. Shish barak is related to both Afghani and Iranian manti and Italian tortellini. Before putting them in warm yogurt, we first bake the dumplings to a crisp in the oven, which is something we learned in Lebanon. Our friend Reem cooks the dumplings directly in the yogurt stew.

Reem's Shish Barak

SERVES 4 TO 6

2 cups (250 g) all-purpose flour

1 small onion

Mild olive oil

5 ounces (150 g) ground lamb

2 tablespoons pine nuts

½ tablespoon cinnamon

½ tablespoon allspice

5 cups (1 kg) Turkish or Greek yogurt (see page 126)

2 tablespoons cornstarch

1 clove garlic

1 tablespoon dried mint

- Gradually add lukewarm water (6 to 8 tablespoons/90 to 120 ml should do) to the flour while kneading until you have a dough with a good consistency. Add a pinch of salt as well. Knead for about 15 minutes, until the dough is smooth and elastic. If the dough is tough to knead, let it rest on the counter for a few minutes before proceeding.

- Mince the onion. Heat a splash of oil in a skillet and fry the onion for 5 minutes. Add the ground lamb, pine nuts, cinnamon, and allspice and cook for another 10 minutes over medium heat. Season with some salt.

- Preheat the oven to 350°F (175°C). Roll out the dough until it's very thin, about ⅓₂ inch (1 mm) thick. Using a glass or a cookie cutter, cut out circles with a 2-inch (6-cm) diameter. Place a teaspoon of ground lamb filling at the center of each circle, and close them

by folding the circles into half-moons. Carefully seal the edges, then fold the pointy ends downward and stick them together. You've created a dumpling resembling a little navel, like a tortellini. Place the little navels on a baking sheet and bake them for about 20 minutes, until light brown.

- In a small saucepan, whisk the yogurt and the cornstarch until smooth; run the garlic through a garlic press and add it to the mixture. Gently warm the yogurt mixture over low heat, whisking constantly; do not let it boil or it will curdle. Season the warm yogurt with the mint and some salt. Ladle the baked dumplings into the yogurt and serve right away. You can also cook the dumplings directly in the yogurt: warm the yogurt, add the dumplings, and let them simmer for 10 minutes.

There is Jewish chicken soup, and then there's Jewish chicken soup. Our friend Shahar's Yemenite version, with its piquant *hawaij* (or *hawayej*) spice-mix (turmeric, cumin seed, cloves, and cardamom) is so good we wouldn't mind eating it every day. This soup should be served the traditional way, with spicy *skhug* (hot sauce) and *hilbe* (fenugreek paste).

Shahar's Yemenite Chicken Soup

With skhug

SERVES 4 TO 6

4 large Yukon gold potatoes

2 red onions

2 tomatoes

½ butternut squash

1 carrot

1 bunch flat-leaf parsley

1 tablespoon black peppercorns

4 chicken thighs, cut in chunks

1 teaspoon sugar

1 tablespoon turmeric

1 tablespoon cumin seed

1 teaspoon cloves

2 cardamom pods

FOR THE SKHUG

3 bunches cilantro

5 cloves garlic

5 red chile peppers

½ teaspoon cumin seeds

2 cloves

Seeds of 1 cardamom pod

• Peel the potatoes and cut into wedges. Cut the onions and tomatoes into wedges. Peel and seed the squash and cut in chunks. Peel the carrot and cut into pieces. Place a bunch of the parsley on the bottom of a Dutch oven, add the peppercorns, and place the pieces of chicken on top, skin side up. Add enough water to cover the chicken. Bring to a boil and skim the foam from the surface. When the soup begins to boil, lower the heat. Add the vegetables, cover the pot, and let simmer for 1 to 1½ hours over very low heat. After 1 hour, add the sugar and season with salt. Crush the turmeric, cumin, cloves, and cardamom seeds with a mortar and pestle. Add to the soup. Cook for another 30 minutes.

FOR THE SKHUG

• Coarsely chop the cilantro and process with a hand blender. Process the garlic with the chile peppers and mix with the cilantro. Crush the cumin seeds together with the cloves and the cardamom seeds and mix with the cilantro. Season with salt. Stored in a clean glass jar in the fridge, skhug keeps for a very long time. The taste is quite intense. Stir 2 tablespoons into the soup. Try it, then add more to taste. Eat the soup with some lahuh (Yemeni flatbread) or another type of bread.

Each year, our friend Mina's quince addiction results in a shelf full of jars filled with homemade quince jam. Besides sharing her wonderful pillows and table (see pages 274–75) with us, for this book she also gave us her recipe for sweet quince tarts.

Mina's Quince Tarts

With almond custard

MAKES 8 TARTS

8 sheets puff pastry, thawed

All-purpose flour for dusting

½ cup (120 ml) tablespoons quince jam

Cinnamon

Butter, for greasing

2 egg yolks, plus whatever you need for brushing

¼ cup (50 g) sugar

¾ cup (180 ml) warm whole milk

⅓ cup (50 g) almond flour, plus extra for dusting

Cointreau or orange blossom water (see page 92)

- Preheat the oven to 400°F (205°C). Place a sheet of puff pastry on a flour-dusted work surface, roll it to a 12-by-12-inch (30.5-by-30.5-cm) square, and cut it in half. Repeat with the remaining pastry (you should have sixteen 6-by-6-inch/15-by-15-cm squares). Spread 8 pieces with 2 teaspoons jam, stopping before the edges. Lightly sprinkle with some cinnamon. Place a second sheet on top of the jam-covered puff pastry and meticulously press down along the edges. Roll up the jam-coated sheets as tightly as possible and cut each roll in half. Butter an eight-hole muffin tin, place both halves of the roll in one of the holes, and press down completely. If you want, you can glaze the dough rolls with a little beaten egg yolk. Bake the pastries for about 10 minutes, until golden brown. Let them cool a bit while you make the almond custard.
- With a whisk or hand blender, beat the egg yolks and the sugar until pale and creamy. Place the bowl over a pan with water heated to just below boil-

ing. Keep stirring and gradually add the warm milk. Gently heat until you get a smooth, creamy custard. Add the almond flour and a generous splash of Cointreau or orange blossom water, to taste. Let cool.

- You could punch a little hole in the unbaked pastries and fill them with custard before baking, but we serve the tarts with the custard on the side, along with a dollop of crème fraîche.

MAKE YOUR OWN QUINCE JAM AND QUINCE NOUGAT

- Peel two quinces and reserve the peels. Cut the fruit into wedges and remove the cores. Combine the quinces in a saucepan with an equal measure of sugar, the juice of one lemon, a splash of water, and a cinnamon stick; add the peels and bring to a boil. Reduce to a thick jam over low heat. For the nougat: Process the boiled peels with an equal measure of salted, roasted nuts. Spoon onto a baking pan lined with plastic wrap and let sit until solid.

This is such a simple recipe, yet it's one of the most surprising dishes we've tasted in a long time. The potatoes are drenched in a delightfully tart gravy (in the Middle East they use bitter oranges for this), and the perfectly tender chicken with sweet garlic falls into the category of irresistible and addictive.

Kamal's Orange Chicken

With garlic and potato

SERVES 4

1 (2- to 3-pound/910-g to 1½-kg) organic chicken

Juice of 5 oranges

Juice of 5 lemons

Olive oil

3 heads garlic

1½ pounds (750 g) Yukon gold potatoes

- Rub the chicken with salt and freshly ground black pepper. Place the chicken in a dish, together with the orange and lemon juice and a generous amount of olive oil. Marinate for several hours (preferably overnight), turning the chicken a few times. Do not discard the marinade liquid.

- Preheat the oven to 400°F (205°C). Break the garlic into cloves and peel them. Quarter the potatoes lengthwise. Place the chicken in a large shallow baking dish or roasting pan and arrange the potatoes and the garlic all around it. Pour the citrus marinade over the chicken. Roast the chicken for 15 minutes. Lower the heat to 350°F (175°C) and roast for another 45 minutes.

- Remove the dish from the oven; place the chicken and potatoes on a platter and cover to keep warm. Strain the citrus juice into a saucepan; bring to a boil and reduce for 5 minutes over high heat. Serve the sauce alongside the chicken and potatoes.

When coated in flour and sesame seeds, these Sudanese falafel maintain their shape perfectly. The addition of fresh herbs like cilantro and dill gives them an herbal infusion that isn't common in Middle Eastern falafel. The zesty peanut sauce with hot peppers and lime juice immediately lets you know that you're in Africa.

Ingmar's Tamaaya

Sudanese falafel

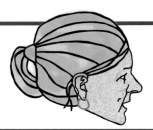

SERVES 4 TO 6 (MAKES ABOUT 24 FALAFEL)

2½ cups (300 g) dried hulled fava beans (available at Middle Eastern grocery stores, sometimes labeled "yellow fava beans")

4 sprigs flat-leaf parsley

1 bunch cilantro

1 bunch dill

2 scallions

1 small onion

2 cloves garlic

½ tablespoon freshly ground pepper

1 tablespoon ground coriander

½ tablespoon chile powder or Aleppo pepper (see page 44)

1½ teaspoons baking powder

7 tablespoons (66 g) white sesame seeds

All-purpose flour for dusting

Peanut oil for deep-frying (aboue 1½ quarts/1.4L)

FOR THE PEANUT SAUCE

1½ cloves garlic

Juice and grated zest of 1 lime

3 green hot peppers

3 tablespoons peanuts

- Simmer the dried fava beans in a pot of water for 10 minutes; they won't be fully cooked, and that's okay. Drain and let cool. Coarsely chop the parsley, cilantro, dill, scallions, onion, and garlic. Add these to a food processor with the fava beans and pulse into a thick puree; if the mixture becomes too dry and grainy, add a splash of water. It should turn into a firm dough. Transfer to a large dish, add the black pepper, coriander, chile powder, baking powder, and a pinch of salt and mix thoroughly. Cover and let rest for 30 minutes.

- For the peanut sauce: Crush the garlic with a mortar and pestle, then add the lime zest. Mince the peppers and add them. Add some salt and finely crush everything into a smooth mixture. Add the peanuts; crush thoroughly until you get a smooth sauce. Add the lime juice and a pinch of salt if you wish. You can also use a hand blender or mini food processor for this.

- Mix the sesame seeds and flour on a flat, rimmed plate. Roll the fava bean mixture into balls the size of walnuts, flatten them, and roll them through the sesame-flour mixture, making sure they're completely covered. In a wok or a deep frying pan, heat the peanut oil to 350°F (175°C) or until a bread cube thrown in instantly turns brown. Working in small batches, deep-fry the falafel for 4 to 5 minutes, until golden brown. Lift them out of the oil with a spider and drain on paper towels. Serve with the spicy peanut sauce.

HOW TO ENJOY AN EFFORTLESS FESTIVE ARABIC MEAL AT HOME

Rule 1

Thoroughly wash your hands before dinner, in case you feel like eating with your hands. This is common in the Maghreb countries, but is frowned upon in the Middle East, where they use flatbread as utensils.

Rule 2

There's always enough for everyone and food is meant to be shared. This means you always cook everything in abundance. After all, there has to be enough food for un-expected guests who show up and leftovers to share with your neighbors (since they've been enjoying all the smells coming from your kitchen), friends, and family. Most dishes taste even better the next day; eating leftovers for lunch the following day is a treat.

Rule 3

Serve the food on a large oval or round dish that leaves enough space around the edges for placing pieces of bread, spoons, and/or forks, so that everybody can join in eating from one communal dish. You eat from the section only directly facing you. The host or hostess can ladle out food from the middle section of the dish and divide it among the guests, making sure everyone has enough.

Decoration

Decoration is important because when you enjoy a meal, all your senses are involved. Drip some rose water on the napkins so the guests can freshen themselves up before dinner. Put candles and small glasses filled with roses in different colors on the table. Leave ample room for the main dish at the center, however, placing it so that every-one can comfortably reach it.

A lot of guests?

If you expect a lot of people over for dinner, arrange a beautiful buffet. Take one spacious table or a low cabinet

After dinner

After the main courses, serve a beautiful bowl filled with freshly washed fruits for everyone to pick and peel. You can also add dried fruits. Serve "white coffee" (hot water for tea, with some orange blossom drops to taste) and Arabian coffee (boiled coffee with cardamom).

No music? No party!

To really set the mood, play some alluring Arabian music. To get you started, we've already made a selection! Kick things off with Fairouz, and if you feel like dancing, you can end the night with Khaled (see page 276).

No large table?

Simply spread a large blanket on the ground, surround it with lots of comfy cushions, and have a "sit-down dinner." Even better—place some small, low tables in the middle of the circle of guests.

Arabian hospitality

"An Arab will always offer his guests the tastiest food and the utmost comfort, even of he has to suffer for it."

Al akl'ala kadd el mahabeh
"Food equals affection"

From: *Food from the Arab World*, by Marie Karam Khayat and Margaret Clark Keatinge

and fill it with bowls and platters of food. It's often a good idea to start with the mezze. Remove empty dishes to keep things moving and to create room for new platters. Liven your buffet by placing roses and candles in between the food dishes. Tip: Use upside-down bowls or platformed cake plates to create different levels; this not only keeps things from getting too crowded, but it also makes your buffet look even more festive.

MUSIC TO ACCOMPANY A
WONDERFUL ARABIAN DINNER PARTY

(Keep an eye on our blog—nadiaenmerijn.nl—and our Facebook page for more suggestions.)

Fairouz is a legendary singer, the ultimate icon of Arabian music. She's especially superb on her latest album, *Eh fi amal*. Mandatory listening!

Ziad Rahbani, Fairouz's son and a marvelous interpreter and composer of Arabian jazz.

Oum Khaltoum and Abdel Halim Hafez—not particularly light fare, but these Egyptian nightingales are a must for those in the know.

With the Dutch Yuri Honing Quartet, Rima Khcheich, Falak, and Orient Express play modern yet melodic and melancholy Lebanese jazz songs.

Patrick Alpha's *Hijazz* is an album oozing with cheerful Lebanese jazz sounds.

Ibrahim Maalouf, a contemporary Lebanese jazz trumpet player.

Toufic Farroukh mixes modern Lebanese jazz with Arabian music.

Mashrou Leila, an amazing Arabian alternative pop group from Lebanon.

Trio Joubran, a Palestinian *oud* (traditional lute-like stringed instrument) group.

Sophia Charai's album *Pichu Pichu* is joyful, upbeat Moroccan pop.

Oum, a contemporary Moroccan singer.

Balkan Beatbox, an Israeli-Palestinian collective making crossover dance music in many different styles.

Jane Birkin's *Arabesque* is a collection of beautiful French-Arabian-inspired tunes.

Souad Massi, a French-Algerian singer-songwriter of achingly beautiful songs.

Natacha Atlas—everything from traditional Arabian to jazz and hip-hop; listen to *Ana Hina*.

Anouar Brahem, the celebrated Tunisian *oud* player, plays a mix of classical Arabian music and classic jazz.

Amine and Hamza, a super-energetic Tunisian jazz duo.

Gilad Atzmon plays Israeli-Arabian jazz; outspoken and original.

Marcel Khalife plays Palestinian classical and Arabian *oud* music and knows how to write a gorgeous song.

No Blues—Dutch-Arabian crossover between blues and Arabian music.

Orchestre National de Barbès play gnaoua-music, a unique style from south Morocco—galvanizing, intoxicating music with unmistakable African rhythms.

Taksim Trio, a Turkish trio playing classical Turkish and Arabian music on traditional instruments.

Cheb Mami play contemporary *rai* music at its best.

Lena Chamamyan, a singer with a wonderful voice. On her album *The Collection*, the Syrian Chamamyan sounds like a slightly less jazzy, more playful Rima Khcheich.

Basel Rajoub, a Syrian trumpet player from the city of Aleppo, plays modern Arabian jazz.

Khaled, like Farouz Cheb Khaled, is a true icon. His music is just as brilliant, but it occupies a place on the opposite end of the spectrum. Khaled is the founding father of the immensely popular *raï* music in Algeria.

• ARABIA MENUS •

Quick and easy menus

- fetteh · herb salad · fruit
- pappardelle Trapanese · watercress salad and yogurt · fruit
- bulgur with fava bean salad · samak harra · fruit
- cauliflower lentil salad · fruit
- Turkish pasta with egg, dill, and sucuk · fruit
- freekeh soup · fruit

Weekend menus

- fava bean salad and belboula meatballs · yogurt with pomegranate
- koshari and herb salad · tahini ice cream
- corn couscous with artichoke · samak harra · pomegranate-rose granita
- potato köfte · vegetable tajine with smen · figs with tahini and white coffee
- roasted potatoes with salsa verde · cauliflower lentil salad · sellou with saffron tea
- fish b'stilla with herb salad · afoosa

- grape leaf packages · maqlooba · pomegranate-rose granita
- cumin fennel fries · chicken with pomegranate and sumac · celery salad · fruit
- Kamal's chicken · roasted potatoes with salsa verde · roasted beets with pomegranate molasses · Arabian tea and coffee

Festive menus

- sucuk-semolina pizzas · roasted eggplant with herbs · Gala's rice with meat · herb salad · tahini ice cream and pomegranate-rose granita · Arabic coffee with pine nut cookies
- labnehs · grape leaf rolls · cauliflower couscous · fish couscous with fennel and orange blossom tomatoes · phyllo dough pastries with mhallabieh · saffron tea with sellou
- hummus with dukkah · dukkah · grape-leaf bundles · yufka rolls · butternut

squash bulgur salad · Mina's quince tarts
- three dips with homemade bread · Yemenite soup · m'hancha
- labnehs · potato kibbeh · quail fesenjan · herb salad · meghli
- wheat salad with hazelnut · artichoke and orange juice dressing · chicken with date-apricot filling · filled dates with Arabic coffee

Sumptuous breakfast menu

various breads · egg with yogurt · lemon and mint · hummus with dukkah · simit with tahini and pekmez · amlou with fresh bread · Arabic coffee and tea and orange-date juice

Lunch menu

egg with yogurt · lemon and mint · bread with za'atar · Palestinian lentils · homemade bread and labneh balls · cucumber orange blossom water

Buffet menus

- sucuk-semolina pizzas · three vegetable dips · cauliflower couscous · zucchini couscous · lamb chops with capers and bread crumbs · pomegranate ice cream
- labneh · labneh balls · grapeleaf rolls · bulgur fava bean salad · cauliflower lentil salad · yufka rolls · tahini ice cream
- spinach pizza · Turkish pasta with chicken and tahini · potato köfte · herb salad · stuffed dates
- börek · dukkah · hummus with dukkah · dried olives · kibbeh naye · grilled eggplant with tahini · fennel cumin fries · poppy seed Bundt cake with rose petal jam and kaymakli

Tea/coffee menu

- sellou with saffron tea · afoosa with white coffee
- rose meringues · poppy seed Bundt cake with rose petal jam and white coffee
- olive oil cake · pine nut cookies with Arabic coffee

• GROCERY STORES •

Aphrodite Greek Imports
5886 Leesburg Pike
Falls Church, VA 22041
703 931-5055

Asadur's Market
5536 Randolph Road
Rockville, MD 20852
301 770-5558

Best Turkish Food
165 Prairie Lake Road,
 Suite G
East Dundee, IL 60118
866 969-3663
bestturkishfood.com

Dayna's Market
26300 Ford Road, Suite 239
Dearborn Heights, MI
 48127
313 999-1980
www.daynasmarket.com

Kalamala
(Online Middle Eastern
 Grocery)
15900 Blythe Street
Van Nuys, CA 91406
855 525-2625
www.kalamala.com

Kalustyan's
123 Lexington Avenue
New York, NY 10016
www.kalyustyans.com

**Mediterranean Bakery (and
 Store)**
3362 Chamblee-Tucker
 Road
Atlanta, GA 30341
770 220-0706
www.mediterranean-bakery
 .com

**Melissa's/World Variety
 Produce**
PO Box 514599
Los Angeles, CA 90051
800 588-0151
www.melissas.com

Penzeys Spices
12001 W. Capitol Drive
Wauwatosa, WI 53222
800 741-7787
www.penzeys.com

Sahadi's
187 Atlantic Avenue
Brooklyn, NY 11201
718 624-4550
www.sahadis.com

Tulumba
129 15th Street
Brooklyn, NY 11215
866 885-8622
www.tulumba.com

Zamouri Spices
1250 N. Winchester Blvd.
Olathe, KS 66061
913 829-5988
www.zamourispices.com

Shamra
(Online market for food
    items and Arabic CDs)
2650 University Blvd.
Wheaton, MD 20902
301 942-9726
www.shamra.com

The Spice House
1941 Central Street
Evanston, IL 60201
847 328-3711
www.thespicehouse.com

• DUTCH DESIGN IN ARABIA AT HOME! •

For our photo styling we've chosen to work with young, talented Dutch designers because we love their work and because it works well with our food!

Dutch design meets Arabia

Mina Abouzahra: www.abouzahra.nl

Imre Bergmann: www.imrebergmann.nl

Ineke Hans: www.inekehans.com

Jansen+Co: www.jansenco.nl

Klaas Kuiken: www.klaaskuiken.nl

Jongh Label: www.jonghlabel.nl

Fenna Oosterhoff: www.fennaoosterhoff.nl

Maaike Seegers: www.maaikeseegers.nl

Quodes / Mara Skujeniece: www.quodes.com / www.skujeniece.com

Celinda Versluis: celindaversluis.blogspot.nl

Marije Vogelzang: www.marijevogelzang.nl

Lenneke Wispelwey: www.lennekewispelwey.nl

Other addresses

Cotta di Mare: www.cottadimare.nl

Household Hardware: www.householdhardware.nl

Jan Willem van Riel: www.destijlbrouwerij.nl

All earthenware on other pages is from our personal collection.

• INDEX •

Syrische koffie met rozen

Tajine met lamsvlees
en gekonfijte sinaasappel

Saffraanatou

Onze culinaire reis - Merijn Tol & Nadia Zerouali
fotografie Sven Benjamins

• ARABIA •

Nadia and Merijn are well-known food writers and recipe developers in the Netherlands, where they specialize in Middle Eastern cuisine. They write for magazines and newspapers including *delicious.magazine*, *VIVA*, *Red*, and many more. They are food entrepreneurs who do an Arabia pop-up restaurant in Amsterdam, Beirut, and other cities, traveling continually between Holland, Morocco, and Lebanon. They have their own Middle Eastern cooking show on foodchannel 24kitchen.

They are the authors of two previous cookbooks, *Arabia* and *Bismilla Arabia*, for which they traveled extensively throughout the Arab world and cooked with local women, their sources of inspiration and information.

www.nadiaenmerijn.nl

bismilla arabia

De keukens van Palestina, Israël, Turkije, Sardinië, Catalonië,
Libië en Algerije – Nadia Zerouali & Merijn Tol

fotografie Sven Benjamins
illustratie en vormgeving Rosa Vitalie

Schelpjes
In saffraan-peterseliebouillon

Jaffa orange salade
Met granaatappel en geweide amandelen

Gegrilde vis
Met labne en tomaat à la Eyal Shani

• SHUKRAN! •

Shukran to everyone who has become a fan of our food over the past few years. It's so nice and extremely gratifying that so many people love our food! Whether you cook at home or join us at one of our pop-up diners, because of you we get to share our food.

Shukran to Sven and Rosa, who are our *Arabia* family and without whom we would never be able to make these books, nor would we want to. Your contributions always result in even more beautiful photos and illustrations, and once again you've outdone yourselves.

Shukran to Hilde, our publisher at Kosmos, who always gives us her unconditional support and who's one of our biggest fans. Shukran to Holly Dolce, our editor at Abrams, for her enthusiasm and support. Shukran to Marleen Reimer for translating our book into English, and to John Gall for such a beautiful US cover.

Shukran to all our friends, colleagues, and family members in the Netherlands and abroad who always devour our Arabia dishes —and who throw elaborate dinner parties at their own homes and share all the culinary details with us afterward.

Shukran to all the wonderful designers who kindly lent us their work. How lovely that many of you came by the studio to take a look, to cook, and of course . . . to eat.

Shukran to Amale and Karima for making sure we crossed our t's and dotted out i's in our Arabian translations.

Shukran to Jan Willem van Riel, for generously opening the doors to his styling warehouse, where he let us browse freely.

Shukran to all the mothers, women, and men in the Arabian kitchens who taught us how to cook, and from whom we continue to learn today, while they in turn learn from us: a delightful exchange that will fortunately never end.

Shukran to Mina Abouzahra for the express delivery of her gorgeous *Gazella* table and her wonderful Moroccan pillows—and for styling our pages.

Shukran to Marije Vogelzang for giving us our very own unique aprons and napkins with pomegranate embroidery—and for coming up with the fantastic slogan "Arabia, edible love." Yes, that's what drives us!

Shukran to 24kitchen and our production team, who've made it possible for us to share our Arabia food with even more people in the Netherlands.

Shukran to our culinary friends Kamal Mouzawak, Ingmar Niezen, Mina Abouzahrab, and Reem Albacha for generously sharing their recipes.